RETAIL BUYING TECHNIQUES

BSSA Guides for Retailers

This book is the latest in the BSSA series of specialist guides for retailers, under the editorship of Peter Fleming, of PFA Business and Personnel Development Consultants.

The series deals with topical issues in retailing today and is growing all the time. The "house style" works towards making the text approachable and enjoyable, supported throughout by checklists, case histories and personal assignments. Each publication has been designed to relate closely to others in the series and all are based on good practice in the Industry.

For further information on the series, or to order further copies, telephone Management Books 2000 on 01285-760722.

BSSA ————————————————————————————

The British Shops and Stores Association (BSSA) plays an important part both in influencing and reflecting the views of the retail industry, with a brief to serve, protect and advance the interests of non–food retailers. In practical terms, that means lobbying both UK and European legislators on a wide range of issues which affect specialist retailers; offering impartial advice on legal, financial and property matters and providing a helpline for day to day business problems.

The Association's training mission is

• to enable retailing firms to achieve productivity, profitability and excellence in customer service through their investment in people;

• to promote and provide the means by which people at all levels in distribution can develop their skills to the limits of their aspirations.

BSSA's commitment to its members does not stop at good advice. With particular expertise in the fields of ladies' and men's fashions, fabrics, general merchandise, furniture, furnishings and carpets, a range of commercial and other services are regularly evaluated and updated. Whether there is a need to increase efficiency and commitment through training, insure the business via BSSA's broking services or save time and money when making regular payments, BSSA has retailers' interests constantly in mind.

Operating in dynamic trading environments, influenced by political, economic, social and technological pressures, retailers today have to respond to constant change. To stay ahead they need timely, accurate and unbiased advice – and BSSA is the first source that many turn to!

Full details of membership and further information on the Association is available from Middleton House, 2 Main Road, Middleton Cheney, Banbury, Oxon. OX17 2TN (telephone 01295–712277 or facsimile 01295–711665).

RETAIL BUYING TECHNIQUES

How to Plan, Organise and Evaluate Retail Buying Decisions AND Improve Profitability

Fiona Elliott and Janet Rider

2000

First published in 2000 by
Management Books 2000 Ltd,
Cowcombe House
Cowcombe Hill
Chalford
Gloucestershire GL6 8HP
Tel. +44 (0) 1285–760722
Fax. +44 (0) 1285–760708
e-mail: MB2000@compuserve.com

Printed and bound in Great Britain by Biddles, Guildford.

British Library Cataloguing in Publication Data is available

ISBN 1–85252–307–7

Preface

Retailing is a fascinating industry. Where else would we find such an intricate network of interlocking roles – and such a rich variety of organisation? The scale of the industry in the UK is awesome, with powerful major retailers but room also for the smaller retailer whose specialisation adds to the rich mix of shopping opportunities.

These variations mean that there will never be just one perfect way of achieving a successful business, still less just one way of organising it. The way in which a retail business organises its buying function is a case in point. In small organisations all the buying may well be carried out by the proprietors themselves; however, as the business grows, there will be an increasing need for a dedicated buying function. But whoever takes responsibility for buying, be it the proprietor or a specialist employed for the purpose, the fundamental challenges and approaches will be similar.

Good buyers who can build the perfect product range for their market are always in demand. Technology and global trading are presenting retailers with unprecedented challenges and buyers are a vital link in ensuring businesses remain profitable in the new millennium.

But where do good buyers come from? Sourcing merchandise for a retail business is a highly skilled profession. The role requires self-confidence, good judgement, balanced risk-taking, as well as the skills of persuasion, leadership and enterprise. Buyers need a breadth of vision – across their own business and that of their suppliers and competitors too.

This book will make an important contribution to the better understanding of any buyer's work making it essential reading for all executives responsible for buying at whatever level.

I wish all readers success in applying the learning to their personal and business growth.

John Hoerner
Chief Executive
The Arcadia Group

CONTENTS

1

What You Will Be Able To Achieve From This Book

1. Introduction

This book has been deliberately written for buyers – but who is a buyer? Retail buying is structured in many different ways as this book recognises in the early chapters. So, the advice we have brought together will be of equal value to:

- central buyers in large retail businesses
- their assistants and deputies
- trainee buyers
- managers – both senior and junior – and anyone else who may have a buying responsibility.

In recognising the variations in style and organisation of the buying function in the industry, we are also addressing a "broad church" – and this should be especially noticeable in the breadth of sophistication in the assignments which are included throughout the book.

Buying is well recognised as a vital function in retailing; it is also an attractive career aspiration for many new entrants into retail businesses. However, advice and formal training are scarce – and even less literature is available which is written from the direct experience of practising buyers! This may have some direct connection with the vulnerability of the role – failure in buying can bring significant performance difficulties in retailing – and this is rarely tolerated by senior managers for very long.

It might seem unfair that those who have received little training might also find themselves seeking another job when performance objectives have not been met, but this is precisely a reason for publishing this book. The aim is simply to make available a body of advice and to give all buyers – experienced and new entrants alike – access to the fundamental buying "facts of life". If we help some achieve greater job security and everyone the means of improving their results and, possibly their career prospects, our mission will have been accomplished!

To date, the book series has concentrated on the customer-facing element of retailing and here we are emphasising the role by which retailers achieve their business objectives. This is not an easy task as any retailer will quickly admit. There have been many well publicised failures in the retail world – born as much through a failure to address the constant need for renewal – as through any endemic risk in a particular sector. Senior management change, buyers change, but the buying and selling process continues. The principal gap between those who become market leaders and the rest is often determined by the quality of the buying team and the marketers, who have correctly identified the firm's special market niche and set about attracting customers in the most professional of ways. The processes involved in sourcing the merchandise may sometimes be taken for granted by any casual observer but, in these days of global economies, strategic trading alliances and brand management, highly skilled buyers with broad experience are not that easy to find.

So, this text should help the reader pursue the self-development task with some vigour! This is not to say that it will replace the training opportunities which may become available. The regular use of Case Histories throughout the book are intended to bring a third dimension to the text and illustrate some of the ways in which the basic principles work in different situations. There is no doubt that greater value will be gained from readers being able to take back the key points of each chapter and find out how they work in their own businesses. There are two ways in which this can be helped:

- through the Assignments which appear in each chapter
- by attending a buying techniques workshop at which supporting coaching and tuition can be provided.

This is not to dilute the importance of obtaining coaching support inside the organisation itself. The old adage, "if you do not understand, just ask" will work very well if we are favoured with the knowledge of the right questions to ask in the first place! This publication should, at the very least, provide a clue to the questions – as well as provide many of the answers.

Throughout each chapter, the reader will be confronted with Key Learning Points which often provide a brief summary of a detailed passage. Armed with these points, the enthusiastic "trainee" may find the basis for a conversation with a mentor in a senior buying position who may be able to invest some time in explaining how the key learning point applies in their firm. So, here is the first key learning point:

The broad principles of retail buying are the same throughout the industry, the methods of application vary somewhat. However, the differences often boil down to system variations – or even just a different vocabulary for the same things!

2. Skills with Things v. People Skills

Buyers are often mesmerised by systems, budgets and products, and it can become easy to forget that the job is just as concerned with people – the customers and their buying habits, and the firm's sales people who are expected to sell the products. It is easy to see how unhealthy "gaps" can open up between the buyer and the finance department on one side and the operations team on the other and this is without any thought for the political intrigues which can be found in some organisations (both large and small). Buyers have to be good with figures and systems – or they will find it increasingly difficult to stay ahead of the race. However, their real success will come when all their suppliers' staff treat the buyer's interests as their top priority, and the sales teams invest all their enthusiasm into selling what has been bought. This does not happen automatically – the achievement comes after the investment of much time and energy in simple things like communications (keeping everyone in the picture!).

All buyers need to remember that good customer relations depend upon good management and staff relations. Buyers need reliable and trustworthy suppliers, and sales people need accessible and communicative buyers!

3. Not Obvious Until Described

The reader may find another challenge in this book – that of reading what might be described as "obvious". If this should happen to you, beware of discarding the "truth" as something you already knew! There are many things that we "know" but choose to ignore or only practice half-heartedly. Readers will have met current or past buyers who scored very successfully on the financial and popularity ratings and yet did not seem to follow any obvious system or formalised approach. Repeated questioning about how they manage this often brings a wry smile and a tongue-in-cheek reference to their long years of experience. The trouble is that experience and luck can help buyers enormously but neither commodity is easily learned by the newcomer – and both may be decidedly missing at the same time with potentially disastrous results.

We unashamedly preach the wisdom of a systematic approach to buying – one which will help reduce some of the more dangerous risks involved in the job. However, the buying operation cannot function in a vacuum – there is a fundamental need for the business to provide a well researched and credible trading policy to guide its buyers and enable them to drive the business forward. This book touches upon these matters but mostly helps readers apply specific techniques in the pursuit of their objectives.

 Buying skills will only be truly effective when they are applied in a business with a clear vision and policy.

The main structure of the text then will guide the reader through the buying process; junior members, or those who are assisting a buyer who relies on instinct may not find all the messages apply to their environment. This should not be a cause for rejecting the advice. There are many routes to profitability and it may be that your organisation has an even better method or approach than those we are advocating!

4. Looking Ahead

The book has been written in 3 parts:

Part 1 – Buying Policy and Structure – explores the processes involved in drawing up Buying Policies within the context of the overall business – a vital topic if buyers are to link their activities into the organisation's business plan.

Part 2 – The Buying Process – analyses the planning stages involved in budgeting for the range and establishing sources of supply for those product lines intended for the firm to offer.

Part 3 – Implementation – offers an examination of the operational tasks which can make or break the success of the buyer's work – and points to areas in which the buyer will have an important input in trying to help the firm achieve maximum results.

The format is deliberately intended to help the reader explore the topics at two different levels – the subjects in logical order (rather as the organisation might) and also in a random, "dippable" fashion, as the need arises.

5. Chapter Overviews

Part 1 will be valuable to the novice who had only a vague idea about business planning in general, and needs to understand the process of forming an appropriate buying and merchandising policy. The section will also be useful to seasoned executives in considering the appropriate structure for buying responsibilities in their firms. In exploring corporate strategy, the topic of market segmentation is described with its application to customer behaviour (chapter 2). Using this base, the text moves on to consider buying policy – and the issues which this should include (chapter 3).

    Part 2 quickly establishes the importance of planning in the buyer's tool-kit with a close look at the steps leading to (and including) the formation of the open to buy budget (chapter 4). Two chapters follow with the framework for the allocation of funds across a range plan (chapter 5) and considering the various sources of supply which the buyer uses (chapter 6). This approach is repeated in chapter 7 which explores the practical processes of range development and range planning – before the analysis of brand development (chapter 8).

    Part 3 then turns to the operational aspects of buying and buyers' influence in reviewing the performance of their parts of the business (chapter 9) with advice on how to contribute to the promotional aspects of trading (chapter 10). Presentation of the product is then considered in a practical review of merchandising from the buyer's standpoint (chapter 11) and the section closes with some valuable advice about how to improve one's own buying performance (chapter 12).

    Successful use of the book, however, will be demonstrated by the reader's ability to interpret each section in his or her own environment – an ability which can help the reader become a real "high flier"!

 Buying remains one of the most attractive roles in the retailing industry; it also contains its own hazards but, with a good grasp of the fundamental techniques, all buyers should be able to achieve success.

Peter Fleming
Series Editor

Checklist

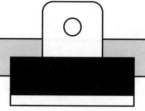

1. The broad principles of retail buying are the same throughout the industry, although the methods of application vary somewhat. However, the differences often boil down to system variations – or even just a different vocabulary for the same things!

2. All buyers need to remember that good customer relations depend upon good management and staff relations. Buyers need reliable and trustworthy suppliers and sales people need accessible and communicative buyers!

3. Buying skills will only be truly effective when they are applied in a business with a clear vision and policy.

4. Buying remains one of the most attractive roles in the retailing industry; it also contains its own hazards but, with a good grasp of the fundamental techniques all buyers should be able to achieve success.

PART ONE

BUYING POLICY AND STRUCTURE

"There is no 'one right way' of structuring the buying function – many organisations have tried to fix things in store and found it necessary to re-organise from time to time. Whatever structure is adopted, buyers need to be supported by clear policies and the freedom to get on with the job – within sensible control mechanisms and shared responsibility."

Peter Fleming
Retail Consultant and Managing Partner
PFA International

PART ONE

BUILDING POLICY AND STRUCTURE

2

Buying and Merchandising In Perspective

1. Introduction

Buying is one of the key functions of a retail business, with the potential to make or break a company. It is, therefore, vital that buyers understand how their role fits within the whole organisation and how the buying activity is able to contribute to the business.

In this chapter we will look at :

- how buying is positioned within most retail organisations
- the development of buying strategy and policy
- how knowledge of the market is a key skill for all buyers and how this creates a framework within which buyers can fulfil their role.

We will go on to consider how buyers can define and know the market in which they operate. The last section will consider the most important people to all buyers' roles – the customers who buy the products they select.

2. Buying Within the Context of the Business

Buying, the selection and purchase of the products which a retailer sells, is usually managed by a specialist team of people. This buying department is commonly one of several departments within a retail company which may also include finance, marketing, human resources and store operations. The following diagram shows a typical structure for a large retailer and the position of buying within that structure. Smaller companies may have scaled-down versions of this structure or, in very small companies, the buying function may comprise part of a director's role or even that of the owner.

Example of a Buying Department Organisational Structure

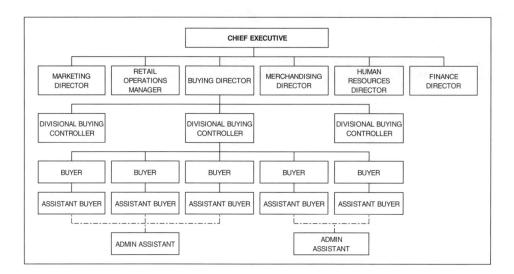

In this example, the buying director reports to the chief executive and has three buying controllers, one for each division of the business. These could be women's fashion, childrenswear and men's fashion. Buyers then report to the divisional controllers, with each buyer having an assistant buyer and shared administrative support. Ten years ago, this level of administrative support would have been much higher, probably one person per buyer. However, with the increased use of computers, many buyers now manage their own administration.

The main variations to this structure lie in the definitions of buying and merchandising. Some companies, particularly traditional department stores, combine these two roles, whereas other companies may sub-divide them further into buying, product development, trading, planning and supply base management, with each section responsible for specific aspects of the "buyer's" role. Whatever structure is adopted, the buyer's role remains vital to the implementation and achievement of the company's key objectives.

 Whatever the size of the business the buying function never operates in isolation from the rest of the business.

3. Corporate Strategy

The primary function of all retailers is to make a profit! Profit normally comes from the products which are sold and it is the role of the buyer to ensure that the correct products are bought which will appeal in sufficient quantity to the customer, so that they can be sold to achieve the company profit targets.

The overall targets for the business form part of its corporate strategy. This strategy defines the key objectives of the business over a set time period, usually between 1 and 5 years and these are often a mixture of financially based and aspirational targets which define the style of the company. Aspirational targets may be separated out and referred to as the Mission Statement. An early example of a mission statement was epitomised by Habitat's slogan "Good design at good prices" – which was also used in marketing products to customers. The mission statement is often stated in the Annual Report and Accounts of the business.

Case History

A soft-furnishing retailer called "Festoons" has the following typical components within its corporate strategy :-

To achieve a sales increase of 10% per annum for the next five years.

To increase the gross margin by 1.2% per annum for the next five years.

To reduce costs by 2% per annum over the next five years.

To increase "Festoons" market share of the furnishings market by 5% within the next two years.

To offer the best choice of home furnishings on the high street.

Assignment 2:1 What is the corporate strategy of your company?

The corporate strategy provides a broad framework for every department within the business to contribute to – from marketing to finance, and from retail operations to buying.

4. Buying Strategy

So how does buying strategy differ from the corporate strategy?

In order to ensure that the strategic goals of the business will be achieved, each sector needs to define its own strategy, targeting its own activities to the attainment of the corporate targets. The buying strategy is the overall plan of what the buying function will achieve in a given time period and how. This strategy is often defined at a senior management level, but in some companies, the buyer's involvement may be sought. This involvement makes it easier for the buyers to implement the strategy, as they will already understand how and why it was created.

The buying strategy will reflect the corporate strategy but it will relate specifically to the buying function with precise and measurable targets. For example, if a company placed considerable emphasis upon marketing its own-brand rather than those of the manufacturer, one element of the buying strategy may be:

- to ensure that 50% of the products bought are own brand merchandise.

Alternatively if the number of suppliers were too large to be manageable, thus impacting upon the efficiency of the buying department, the buying strategy may include:

- to reduce the supply base by 20% over a 3 year period.

The first of these points would support a corporate strategy of improving gross margin as, on average, gross margin is normally higher on own-label merchandise than on branded goods. The second strategy, of reducing the supply base, would help with the reduction of costs within the business. The operation of each supplier account is a cost to the business and, if the supply base can be rationalised, costs of communication and administration can be reduced. For this reason, the reduction of the supply base is a common buying strategy. A smaller supply base may also concentrate more business through less supply companies, providing the buyer with increased negotiating power with which to reduce cost prices. However, there are risks involved in reducing the supply base such as becoming over-reliant upon a few suppliers.

As well as providing targets for the buyers, the buying strategy creates a framework within which the buyers can work, by defining the company's policy or approach to the many aspects of buying.

For example, the policy on visual merchandising may state that all products must be packaged in boxes carrying the retailer's name and to a design set out in the packaging guidelines. This policy could directly relate to the company's strategy of promoting own-label merchandise to reinforce brand identity and to maximise its appeal to the target customers.

The following diagram using the example of a hosiery retailer called "Legs Eleven", illustrates how the buying policies relating to price and suppliers were developed from the Mission Statement and the corporate strategy. Sometimes these are not referred to as policies but tend to be "ways of doing things" – which buyers learn. However, this approach fails to ensure that the policies are considered within the framework of the buying strategy, and can result in an inconsistent approach.

The Creation of Buying Strategy and Buying Policy

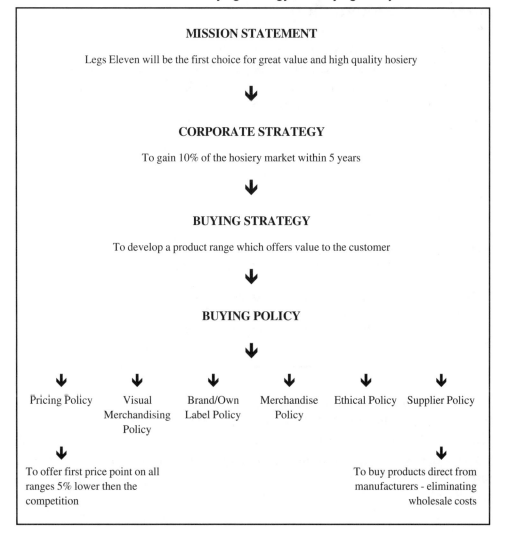

MISSION STATEMENT

Legs Eleven will be the first choice for great value and high quality hosiery

⬇

CORPORATE STRATEGY

To gain 10% of the hosiery market within 5 years

⬇

BUYING STRATEGY

To develop a product range which offers value to the customer

⬇

BUYING POLICY

⬇

⬇	⬇	⬇	⬇	⬇	⬇
Pricing Policy	Visual Merchandising Policy	Brand/Own Label Policy	Merchandise Policy	Ethical Policy	Supplier Policy

⬇

To offer first price point on all ranges 5% lower then the competition

⬇

To buy products direct from manufacturers - eliminating wholesale costs

The subject of buying policy is covered in more detail in Chapter 3. However, any policy within the business should ultimately relate back to the buying strategy and, in turn, the corporate strategy. However many business policies exist because "that's how it has always been done", "it is how the competition do it" or "someone senior thought it was *a good idea*", a more effective approach is to consider the aims and objectives of the business and then decide on the best course of action.

 Buying is far more effective if it is focused on the achievement of business objectives and on the customer who will ultimately buy the products.

5. Market Segmentation

Every business and every buyer works within a specific market sector, e.g. lighting, lingerie, frozen desserts. It is part of the buyers' jobs to understand the markets to ensure that their buying is effective. Some markets may appear easy to define, but others are less clear as the following example illustrates.

Case Example

What market am I in?

In the 1950s, an American called Theodore Levitt published an article called "Marketing Myopia". In it he challenged companies' perceptions of their market.

Taking the American railways as an example he disputed that their market was railways, instead he redefined it as "transport". Suddenly the railways were seen as being in competition not only with other railways, but also with road and air transport.

This thought process can be transferred to any business, for example, for the frozen desserts buyer at the supermarket, the market is not just frozen desserts it is all the possible options for dessert from an apple to a fresh gateaux that a customer looking for a pudding could purchase. The buyer's range will need to compete with all these other options if it is to be successful.

Assignment 2:2 *Taking your own market or product sector, try to define what the broader market is.*

Does this change who you regard as your competitors?

---

6. The Market

Having defined the market in its broadest sense, it is vital if you are to be successful as a buyer that you learn everything about that market.

 Knowledge of the market ensures that the buyers have detailed information on which to base their buying decisions. Informed decisions are better decisions.

Market research companies may have been commissioned by your company to produce reports on the relevant markets but, as this is very costly, it is worth remembering that copies of market sector reports (by organisations such as Keynote) are held at most major libraries.

Market sector reports will provide information on :

- the market size
- the current trends both in size and broad product types
- information on the market share of major retailers or types of retailer (e.g. variety stores or independents).

Despite their general usefulness, two criticisms can be cited at such reports. Firstly, market sector reports are always produced retrospectively so will always be slightly out of date. (However, they do provide a good overview of the market and usually contain a section on predicted future trends). Secondly, the data is not always accurate. Many companies who compare their known turnover with that detailed in a market research report will find discrepancies. However the information is usually sufficiently accurate to be able to identify the general position of a company in the market place.

Trade Sources

Most trade sectors have magazines and journals which provide news and information on the market, and details of the key companies which are active within that market. These will frequently report on market trends, the size of the market and the share taken by the main companies or sectors which contribute to the market.

Many market sectors also have a trade association which can provide information on their particular market sector. This may include trends within the market or current key issues. For example, BSSA provides information to its members on industry news and relevant government reports.

Suppliers can also provide an invaluable source of information on the market and many of them have much longer experience of the market than the buyer. Most suppliers sell products to other retailers and can gain a knowledge of whether the sector is performing well or badly, and which products, colours, materials or finishes are selling well in the market place. Buyers may, or may not, choose to act on the information, but at least they will do so knowing what is happening in their market.

Suppliers can also provide invaluable information on competitors. Some suppliers may give little away, whilst others can be persuaded to convey considerable information. One word of caution however – if they talk about your competitors to you, what do they tell your competitors?

Talk to Your Customers

Many buyers in large businesses spend very active working days in head office and at their suppliers, but seldom (or never) go into their stores and talk to staff and customers. Yet these customers are the very people expected to buy the firm's products. Regular visits to stores can enable buyers to hear customers' views first-hand, and also to hear the views of the sales staff who actually sell the product range.

 One afternoon talking to customers can greatly influence the way a buyer perceives the market and the product range.

However, buyers should be careful not to over-react to the assertive views of one individual, but should consider their findings in the context of their own knowledge of the market.

> ### *Assignment 2:3 Use the following questions in store to find out what the customer thinks about the product range :-*
>
> Could you find the products that you wanted? If not what would you like to see?
>
> Do you think the products are fairly priced?
>
> What attracted you to the products?
>
> Are you a regular shopper with XXX?
>
> Where else do you shop?
>
> Have you bought products from XXX in the past? If yes were you happy with the purchase?

7. The Competition

A key part of knowing the market is being able to recognise competitors and to monitor their activity. So who are *your* competitors? The answer may be fairly straightforward to a multiple retailer, as other multiple retailers are easy to identify, but this may not provide the whole picture. An excellent independent designer clothing shop could provide competition for a multiple retailer in one key location. Obviously this would not affect the whole chain but may require specific measures to be taken in that one location. For example, ensuring that the designer ranges are prominently located and always well merchandised.

New companies in new locations may not be so aware of their competition. In some instances where the location is well-known, such as Regent Street in London, market reports may exist which discuss the profile of retailers and customers. However, in most cases such information will not be available, and the only option – for which there is no real substitute – is to go and look.

These competitor reviews are an important part of learning about a market, they are also an essential element in the buyer's role! Buyers should be in their competitors' stores at least once a month and know their competitors' ranges as well as their own. In addition, competitor reviews provide the opportunity to see new product introductions, promotional activity, display methods, compare key price points and note what stock has been marked down. All this is valuable information when it comes to developing and managing a product range.

Know as much about your competitors as your customers. Customers do not look at your product range in isolation, neither should the buyer.

Assignment 2:4 Complete a SWOT Analysis

A SWOT analysis is a commonly used technique amongst retailers which allows the current state of the business to be evaluated. SWOT stands for Strengths, Weaknesses, Opportunities and Threats. The table below gives an example of a SWOT analysis on a competitor to a newsagent. Strengths and Weaknesses focus on the competitor and Opportunities and Threats concentrate on the opportunities and threats they create for your business.

Strengths	*Weaknesses*
Low prices	Limited product range
Good quality	Poor housekeeping
Strong seasonal promotions	

Opportunities	*Threats*
Offer broad range of products	Review retail prices
Ensure good visual merchandising	

Carry out a SWOT analysis on your 3 key competitors, concentrating on product selection, prices and visual merchandising. Identify their strengths and weaknesses and the opportunities and threats which they represent to your company.

---

8. The Customer

The customer should be the focus of all the buyer's activities, as it is only by meeting the needs of the customer that the business will achieve its financial objectives. Retailing history is littered with examples of retailers who forgot to retain customer focus. Ratners, Laura Ashley and Saxone are three well-known names who lost sight of the needs of their core customers.

Make the customer the central focus for all buying decisions.

Who Is the Customer?

If buyers are to focus on their customers, they must first identify who they are. Indications can be given from what they buy in terms of type of product, price and volume. Supermarkets are currently using loyalty cards to identify which products are bought by customers and to direct specific promotions to particular groups of customers. Unfortunately such sales-based analysis concentrates on the customer a retailer has **today** and not necessarily the customer they will have **tomorrow.**

Market research companies can conduct exit interviews with customers to gain a general view of customer profile and their impressions of your company and its product range. Alternatively, they can conduct more in-depth focus groups which provide a greater insight into customers' profiles or their views. Some retailers are very pro-active in this field with some fashion companies defining their customers down to the level of one individual, giving him or her a name, job, family, leisure activities and income. Whilst this can help the buyer to focus their product range on the customer, it can also prove too specific and lead to the alienation of any customer who does not quite fit the mould. This may result in the customer base becoming too small and a subsequent failure to generate the necessary sales turnover.

Defining Customer Types

Whilst it can be difficult to define a single type of customer, some companies (particularly variety chain stores or department stores with wider product ranges) may have several different types of customer. In order to ensure that they meet the needs of all customers, broad profiles can be created, either by age or sex, or more frequently by lifestyle. A lifestyle profile would group people of the same social and economic characteristics, values, motivations and experience. The "YUPPY" (Young, upwardly mobile, professional person) and the "DINKY" (Dual income, no kids yet) are probably the most well-known examples of a lifestyle category. Socio-economic groups categorise people by their income and social standing and this approach has been widely used for many years.

Socio-Economic Groups

	Head of household's occupation	Social
A	Professionals/Senior Management	Upper middle class
B	Middle Management	Middle class
C1	Supervising or Junior Management	Lower middle class
C2	Skilled Manual Workers	Skilled working class
D	Semi and unskilled Manual Workers	Working class
E	Pensioners, Casual or Lowest Grade Workers	Lowest levels of subsistence

---

However, categorising people by "class" is increasingly beginning to appear an inappropriate and shallow method of classification and lifestyle classifications are often preferred.

Such groupings of customers obviously leads to generalisation, but they do allow for greater targeting of product ranges, whilst retaining a structure which is manageable. It would be impossible to effectively manage a range to satisfy 100 different customer profiles – even four takes a considerable amount of skill, but it *is* possible.

Case History

For example, a garden centre decided to target three different customer profiles:

- couples with young families
- new gardeners
- pensioners with gardens

Their product range included low price garden equipment, labour saving tools, practical textbooks, all weather garden furniture and garden games. Large or expensive garden tools and exotic plants were not stocked. Whilst the keen or experienced gardener was not satisfied with the range, the garden centre enjoyed excellent growth from its three target customer groups. Meanwhile another garden centre 10 miles away, closed within six months after trying to offer too broad a range of products. New gardeners were daunted by the vast array of equipment, experienced gardeners felt that the expensive tools were devalued by the cheaper merchandise and young families lacked the time and the patience to go through the whole range.

The customer focused product range will not attract all your target customers, but it will attract a considerably higher percentage than the unfocused product range and lead to higher sales.

9. Summary

In this chapter, we have considered the role of buying within the context of a retail business, the development of buying strategy and policy and the framework that this creates for the buyer. We also considered the market within which the buyer operates and the customer who is key to the success of any buyer. These issues will be expanded in the next chapter by the exploration of a company's buying policy and its influence on the relationships with its buyers, suppliers, customers and the community at large.

A retail business can respond to changing customer requests on a daily or weekly basis but the real success comes from customers visiting in the knowledge that they will find what they want *when* they want it!

Checklist

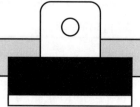

1. Whatever the size of the business, the buying function never operates in isolation from the rest of the business.

2. The corporate strategy provides a broad framework for every department within the business to contribute to – from marketing to finance, and from retail operations to buying.

3. Buying is far more effective if it is focused on the achievement of business objectives and on the customer who will ultimately buy the products.

4. Knowledge of the market ensures that the buyers have detailed information on which to base their buying decisions. Informed decisions are better decisions.

5. One afternoon talking to customers can greatly influence the way a buyer perceives the market and the product range.

6. Know as much about your competitors as your customers. Customers do not look at your product range in isolation, neither should the buyer.

7. Make the customer the central focus for all buying decisions.

8. The customer-focused product range will not attract all your target customers, but it will attract a considerably higher percentage than the unfocused product range and lead to higher sales.

3

Buying Policy

1. Introduction

In this chapter we are going to examine Buying Policy, its key elements and scope, and how it impacts on day to day buying activity. We will consider how a company's buying policy influences its relationships with its buyers, suppliers, customers and the community at large. We will also consider how it influences and shapes the product offering to the customer.

A company is an entity in law and, as such, it interacts with other groups in society. Just like an individual, the company has a set of values, a moral framework. The company defines and demonstrates these values and thereby, its corporate personality through its policy initiatives.

Company Relationships

Firstly, let's take a look at the company's relationship with the buyers themselves.

2. The Buyer

Buyers are often seen as the profit generators of a retail organisation. They do, after all, negotiate the cost prices and fix the selling prices of the merchandise. How much influence, if any, they can have on the formulation of the buying strategy which guides their activities, will depend on the structure of the organisation and the way it operates. The buyer's position in the organisation and the scope of their responsibility indicates their relationship with the company. The company's relationship with its buyers will reflect in the way objectives are set, and to what extent there is real accountability. Is the personal performance of the buyer measured against stated targets or objectives? Are the buyers *really* held accountable for achieving results? More fundamentally, company attitude on the concept of accountability illustrates the relationship between employer and employee.

The company's relationship with its buyers will also reflect in the training and development programmes that are made available. There is more on this subject in our final chapter.

3. Supply Base

Every retailer will have a list of suppliers; they could be manufacturers, importers or wholesalers. They collectively form the "Supply Base". It is the company's buying policy that determines whether the organisation will be dependant on a few suppliers to whom it is very important, or whether it prefers to spread its spend more thinly around several suppliers.

There are advantages and disadvantages in both extremes of policy.

A Narrow Supply Base

The average spend with each supplier will be high. This gives the buyer "important customer status" and therefore, in theory, better buying terms. A real working partnership can be developed more easily when there are just a few suppliers and the administration costs in managing the accounts will be low. However, if the service fails, an alternative source may be difficult to find. It will be more difficult to replace a supplier who supplies a wide range of products.

A Broad Supply Base

The average spend with each supplier will be small. This may place the buyer at a disadvantage in getting the best terms. It will be more time consuming, and more difficult, to develop partnerships with a lot of suppliers where the financial commitment with each of them is low. The administration costs associated with a long list of supplier accounts will be high. However, a broken supply chain may be easier to fix where the buyer is less dependent on any one individual supplier for a large proportion of the product range.

HOW MANY SUPPLIERS?	ADVANTAGES	DISADVANTAGES
FEW SUPPLIERS	High spend per supplier: important customer status Lower administration costs More manageable supply chain Conducive to partnership	High dependence: high stock-out risk Hard to replace if service fails
MANY SUPPLIERS	Low dependence Low stock-out risk Easier to replace if service fails	Low spend per supplier: low customer status High administration costs Less manageable supply chain Less conducive to partnership

The most common solution lies somewhere between these two extremes, with a tendency towards fewer suppliers.

 The emphasis today, is on establishing working partnerships with suppliers, sharing management information and working together in areas of common interest, such as stock delivery, distribution, promotions and in-store stock availability.

Trading terms are at least, influenced if not determined by buying policy. Supplier terms could include such things as:

- settlement discounts and payment period
- off-invoice discounts on invoice totals
- retrospective discounts
- deferred payment terms

- payment of, or a contribution to, staffing costs
- provision of, or a financial contribution towards, fixturing
- advertising contributions
- promotional support, e.g. supply of free gifts for a gift-with-purchase promotion.

Some of these may be fixed, non-negotiable pre-conditions for a trading relationship, set out within a trading terms document whilst others may be left to buyer negotiation.

 A standard "terms of supply" contract, drawn up by the retailer, is quite common. It can make life easier for the buyer at the initial negotiation stage.

The contract will set out what each party is expected to do for the other in the relationship and will typically include such things as:

- settlement discount and payment period
- packaging and labelling requirements
- delivery arrangements (addresses, booking-in procedures, etc.)
- procedures relating to short deliveries, returns and refused goods
- invoicing arrangements (addresses, documentation details)
- ownership of goods.

Assignment 3:1 To help clarify your existing policy and identify any gaps, complete our Policy Issues Action Plan – Supply Base.

This will reveal:

- Your supply base policy

Is there a long list of suppliers with a low average spend, or just a few with a high average spend?

- Your terms of supply

Does your organisation have a standard "terms of supply" contract that it requires its suppliers to sign and abide by? Get a copy and review it. Is it up to date, and does it cover all that it should?

Trading terms represent the "nuts and bolts" of the relationship and may be clearly laid out in a terms document, but what about the quality of the relationship, what influence does buying policy exert here?

Policy Issues Action Plan			
Supply Base	**What is your current policy?** Is it formally written down, or just informally understood?	**What actually happens now?** Does practice comply with policy?	**Action** What needs to be done to bring practice into line with policy?
1. How many suppliers do you have? Examine the supplier list for your business. Which supplier policy is evident? Is there a long list of suppliers, each with a low average spend, or just a few with a high average spend?			
2. Do you have a contract terms of supply document? Does your organisation have a standard contract terms of supply document that it requires its suppliers to sign and abide by? Get a copy and review it. Is it up to date? Does it include all that it should?			

The company expresses its corporate personality through its supplier relationships.

Buying Policy will lay down some guidelines on the quality of the trading relationship for the buyer to follow.

- Will it be an adversarial relationship or a partnership?
- Are you (the buyer) expected to push for the lowest price at all costs?
- Or, are you encouraged to develop a good long-term business partnership?

The latter is much more common these days. Retailers realise that a supplier whose profit margins are squeezed too hard will eventually go out of business and no longer be there to support them.

 A good supplier relationship is one that is effective for both parties. In other words, a good supplier relationship is one that works!

One of the key issues covered by policy, which affects dealings with suppliers, is the acceptance of gifts. When does the acceptance of gifts constitute unethical behaviour?

In some organisations, policy will determine that no gifts may be accepted under any circumstances. In other organisations, a limited range of acceptable gifts may be listed for the employee. These lists will usually include things like pens diaries, etc., items of nominal value, often personalised with the supplier's name.

 Whatever the company policy, remember that, as a buyer, your reputation goes with you from job to job. When you are offered a gift, always ask yourself what motivates the supplier to make the offer and what might motivate you to accept?

4. Community Issues

What relationship does the retailer have with the community?

There is a whole range of issues of interest and relevance to the wider community that are covered by buying policy and which govern buying activity.

We can classify them under the following headings:

- Political
- Social
- Moral
- Health
- Environmental

Let's examine each of these areas individually.

Political

Is the retailer prepared to buy goods from countries whose politics conflict with their own cultural or ethical values? If the answer is yes, then the retailer will be seen to be supporting that regime. It will then have to deal with any adverse publicity it may receive and face criticism from the community. The community, after all, is made up of customers, current or potential!

Social

The exploitation of workers prevalent in certain countries and within certain areas of product manufacture in particular, will be a deterrent to some retailers when sourcing their products.

Case History

The use of child labour in India is quite common. Within Indian society the children are often expected to contribute to the family income. However, a distinction must be drawn between child labour, which is part of Indian society and child bonded labour where children are sold by their parents, to manufacturers, for relatively small sums of money.

One of the trades that use child labour is rug making. In the late 1970s, a rug importer and a group of carpet retailers joined forces with the aim of addressing the issue. Retailers that bought rugs that were produced using child bonded labour faced a moral dilemma – should they buy a product, which was attractive to the consumer, but which, supported the exploitation of children? The retailers, addressed the issue by introducing a scheme into which money was donated, that enabled the children be bought out of bondage and provided them living accommodation, education **and** work – making rugs. This allowed the children to attend school **and** receive a financial award for their efforts.

In the late 1980s, the Anti-Slavery League took action and introduced a rug mark which can only be attached to rugs that do not use child bonded labour in their manufacturing process. This "seal of approval" is still in use today.

There are, of course, many positive initiatives that have social implications of interest to the community, the "Books for Schools" promotional initiative, for instance, adopted by the major supermarkets. This promotion involved the customer receiving vouchers on their purchases, which could be exchanged for books when donated to a local school.

Moral

The buying and selling of animal fur products raises the moral question of whether it is right to kill animals for their fur. The testing of beauty products on animals raises consumer objections and stimulates public debate. But it also raises another question about choice. Should the retailer take a moral stance by making the decision to refrain from offering certain products for sale, or include products in the range and leave it to the customer to decide whether or not to buy? It does pose the question – retailer or moral guardian?

Case History

Body Shop has made very clear its position on the testing of beauty and skin-care products on animals and has successfully marketed itself as a morally and

---

Health

"Alcopops" as they quickly became known, caused a stir when they were launched onto the drinks market. These were a new breed of sweet, mildly alcoholic, fizzy drinks. Their bright, stylish packaging, it was alleged, was designed to attract children and teenagers and this raised both moral and health issues. Some retailers banned them from sale.

Environmental

The extensive use of plastic carrier bags, particularly by the food supermarkets, led to a number of positive initiatives. These initiatives arose in response to the pressure exerted by environmental groups who expressed concern at the growing use of landfill sites for waste disposal. The supermarkets responded with a number of re-cycling initiatives.

The ethical stance taken by the retailer, and reflected in its buying policy, will influence and guide the buyer's product sourcing, ranging and buying decisions.

Assignment 3:2   Now complete our Policy Issues Action Plan – Ethical Issues

What is your company policy on ethical issues?

Policy Issues Action Plan

Ethical Issues	What is your current policy? Is it formally written down, or just informally understood?	What actually happens now? Does practice comply with policy?	Action What needs to be done to bring practice into line with policy?
1. Political			
2. Social			
3. Moral			
4. Health			
5. Environmental			

5. Customer Issues

Who is your customer? As discussed in the previous chapter, it is important to know who your customer is! Market research can provide many of the answers. It can define your customer profile quite precisely by a variety of means.

Demographics

This term is used to describe and define the age profile of the population.

The Government's Central Statistical Office produces figures based on Census, birth and death rate information, including, for example, the following.

- Will the proportion of the population over retirement age grow, or decline, in the next 10 years?
- Will the number of children entering primary school education grow, or decline, over the next 5 years?

Demographic profiling and forecasting provides some answers. But what relevance has this to you, the retailer? You need to know if your customer base is going to decline over the long (or short) term? If so, what strategies will you put in place to ensure your economic survival?

Having identified who your customer is, there may be many reasons, other than demographic, why you could want to change your customer base. It may be felt that attracting a different type of customer will bring greater opportunities for business growth. Buying policy will define your target customer. This may be the same as, or different to, your existing customer profile.

If a retailer wants to change its customer profile, it may have to change its name, its image, its level of customer service, its product range, or all of these things!

Evolution or Revolution?

Will the change take the form of an overnight transformation? A branch closure, refurbishment and a re-launch? Or, will the transformation be accomplished gradually, over an extended period of time so that existing customers hardly notice the changes taking place?

Case History

Heinz baked beans packaging has been changed many times over the last 30 years, but on each occasion, the changes have been slight, resulting in a change over the years that has largely gone unnoticed by the consumer. In this way, brand recognition has been preserved.

The softly, softly approach involves carrying your existing customers along with you, perhaps while a new customer base is being established. Revolutionary change is usually a costly, high-risk strategy. Neither strategy provides an easy solution or can guarantee success.

The transformation of Chelsea Girl to River Island provides a good example of revolutionary change.

Case History

Chelsea Girl was a fashion multiple, at its peak in the 1970s, that sold high fashion clothing primarily for the teenage market. As the population profile began to change, the chain began to suffer. Overnight, or so it seemed, the Chelsea Girl name disappeared, and in its place River Island appeared. River Island by comparison, was an altogether more sophisticated retail concept, aiming at a slightly older and more sophisticated customer probably between 18 and 35 years. The images of these two fashion shops were very different, and in the eye of the consumer there was no connection between them. River Island presented itself as a totally new business.

Customer Service

The level of customer service may seem at first to be a purely operational issue, but it has major implications for the buying team.

Personal service or self-selection?

If a business decides to follow a policy of customer self-selection, rather than seeking to provide the customer with staff who are available to give help and advice, then the product packaging and point of sale material will be critically important as the silent salesmen of the product. Everything the customer is likely to need to know must be communicated visually.

When we think of customer service, it is probably the lack of it that immediately springs to mind!

Complaints Policy

Company policy on the handling of customer complaints is of particular relevance to the buyer in their dealings with suppliers. Some customer complaints will be resolved by the retailer without recourse to the supplier. But, many types of complaint will involve the buyer and supplier in some way. In order to examine this further we need to ask what customers complain about. Why do they return goods and seek an exchange or a refund?

Let's look at some of the most common reasons:

- *Product quality*
  The products we sell should, of course, be "of merchantable quality". This is a legal requirement. In cases of questionable product quality, the customer may have rejected the goods because of a manufacturing fault or damage sustained at some stage during or after manufacture. In any event, the sale transaction is between the retailer and the customer and it is the retailer's responsibility to satisfy the customer. Any cost in doing this will initially be borne by the retailer. Having satisfied the customer, it is usually the buyer (as the retailer's representative) who will take the matter up with the supplier and seek to pass on any appropriate proportion of the cost of resolving the complaint. If the product was damaged after manufacture, the supplier is unlikely to stand any of the cost, unless the damage was sustained during handling and the cause was found to be poor packaging. In this situation the supplier might accept some responsibility.
  (The BSSA book entitled "Law for Retailers" gives further insight into these issues.)

- *Wrong size or poor fit*
  If a customer buys a garment that fails to meet the sizing requirement, this is usually something that the buyer will take up with the supplier. The garment or batch of garments may simply have been incorrectly labelled (a size 10 dress with a size 12 label!) or, the garments may fail to conform to the size specification agreed by the buyer. This will usually mean returning goods to the supplier.

- *Late delivery*
  Where goods are made-to-order for the customer, and a delivery date is quoted, there will always be a risk of late delivery, which may lead to cancellation of the order. Things like furniture and made-to-measure curtains are obvious examples. Where a supplier is repeatedly failing to

"deliver", the buyer is likely to get involved. The trading relationship with that supplier would come under increasing pressure with each delayed order. Ultimately, the buyer may cease trading with the supplier and find an alternative source of supply for the product or product range.

How important is good customer service? How far is the company prepared to go to satisfy the customer? How much will it cost? Here is the profit vs. service dilemma.

It can prove very costly to resolve some customer complaints. However, it can prove even more costly to fail to resolve the complaint!

The saying "Bad news travels faster than good news" is certainly true where shopping experiences are concerned. The retailer has to weigh up the alternatives. Is it cheaper to satisfy the customer than to risk the damage that would be sustained by bad publicity? Can the business afford to lose the good will of even one customer? The answer is usually "NO".

Assignment 3:3 Now complete our Policy Issues Action Plan –
Customer Issues

1. Does your buying policy define who your target customer is?

2. What is your company policy on customer complaints?

Policy Issues Action Plan

Customer Issues	What is your current policy?	What actually happens now?	Action
	Is it formally written down, or just informally understood?	Does practice comply with policy?	What needs to be done to bring practice into line with policy?
1. Who is your target customer?			
2. How do you handle customer complaints?			

5. Promotion Policy

If the business has an image of aggressive discounting, then the buying activity will centre on the procurement of competitively priced special purchases or "deals". Where the business is less aggressively promotional, the buyer will give more attention to creating and maintaining regular product ranges. These are the extremes and the promotional policy will usually be somewhere in between.

Buyers not only have to fulfil the requirements of the range structure plan (see chapter 5) but they will also have to buy product to support the promotional programme. The promotion calendar will set out the planned promotional activity for the trading period. When the promotion plan is created well in advance of the trading period, the buyer can similarly forward-plan promotions with suppliers. Where a true partnership exists, there will usually be co-operation and often practical supplier support in terms of funding, with money being allocated from the suppliers' promotional budget. Supplier funding could present itself in many forms:

- wholly, or partly, funded advertising
- product discounting
- provision of staffing for in-store demonstrations, or contribution to staffing costs.

 Planned promotional activity can be built into the buying plan. But, unplanned promotional activity can create problems for the buyer.

A spur-of-the-moment decision to hold a "20% off" weekend could have a seriously detrimental effect on gross profit if the resultant sales volume increase fails to meet expectations. (More on this subject later in chapter 10, Promotions and Profitability).

6. Pricing Policy

Pricing Policy is encompassed within Promotional Policy and directly influences the buyer's decisions on pricing in 3 main areas:

Price Pointing

Round pounds or 99p price endings? Does £4.99 sound cheaper than £5? Is £1000 a more acceptable price point than £999.99?

Should a multi-product retailer, like a department or chain store, adopt a different policy in different product areas within the store, or should there be a consistency of approach throughout the store?

Single and Dual Pricing

Dual pricing a product should enhance the customer's belief that they are getting real value for money – but are they?

The big debate is whether the comparisons can really withstand scrutiny. Price comparisons have to comply with standards laid down by law.

 Compliance with the letter of the law does not automatically mean compliance with the spirit of it!

How reliable and honest is the comparison? It may comply with the 28-day rule that stipulates that a product should have been on sale at the higher price for at least 28 consecutive days prior to the Sale offer, but did the retailer genuinely expect to sell any product at the full price of £19.99?

Dual pricing is used extensively by some retailers all year round, whereas others use it more selectively at Sale periods, perhaps only twice per year. Single pricing relies on the product appearing worthy of its price on its own merits, with no price comparison shown.

Price comparison operates not just within a store on a particular product, as in the case of dual pricing, but between competing retailers when customers shop around.

How will the retailer respond to price competition?

Price Matching

There may be a policy of price matching in place, which promises to match the price of any product seen elsewhere at a lower price within a specified time period. This is provided, of course, that the customer's claim can be substantiated. "Double the difference" promises have been made in the past, but are rarely seen now. These promises can obviously have a considerable impact on the profit margin. In these circumstances, there is pressure on the buyer to try to ensure that prices will not be undercut and, in the event that they are, the overall margin for the product area or department must be able to support the cost of the price match.

Assignment 3:4   Now complete our Policy Issues Action Plan – Pricing Policy

What is your company policy on pricing and promotions?

Policy Issues Action Plan

Pricing Policy	What is your current policy? Is it formally written down, or just informally understood?	What actually happens now? Does practice comply with policy?	Action What needs to be done to bring practice into line with policy?
1 Price Points What price points are in use - round pounds or 99p endings?			
2. Price Matching Do you operate a policy of price-matching your competitors' prices?			

7. Merchandise Assortment

If you were confronted with 40 different irons to choose from, would you have the patience to follow a decision making process that would eventually lead you to select and buy just one?

As customers, we want to have a choice, but too much choice causes confusion.

 More product options don't always mean more choice!

Width of merchandise assortment is something that is covered by Buying Policy and is defined in the range structure plan, which we will consider in detail, in chapter 5.

Real choice requires that each product in the range should have something uniquely different to offer the customer. This is often referred to by the term "USP" which stands for "Unique Selling Proposition". From the retailer's point of view, the range should have maximum customer appeal, with the lowest possible number of product options. In other words, ***the best possible choice with the lowest possible stock investment.***

Consider the specifications scheduled on page 49. There are a total of 40 different models of iron with prices ranging from £8.95 to £99.00. If this range were to be rationalised, which models would be taken out? How would the buyer decide which models to keep in the range and which to reject?

Irons Range

Ref No	Brand	Product	Selling Price	PRODUCT FEATURES							
				Travel Iron	Dry Iron	Steam	Spray	Jet of Steam	Boost of Steam	Coloured	Cordless
1	Jarini	JR47	4.99		●	●					
2	Jarini	JR69	8.99	●	●	●					
3	Jarini	JR15X	11.99		●	●	●				
4	Merrington	MT234	12.25	●	●	●	●				
5	Jarini	JR48	12.75		●	●	●	●			
6	Richard Peters	RP1520	12.80	●	●						
7	Richard Peters	RP4500	12.99		●	●					
8	Daniels	D220	17.99		●	●	●				
9	Richard Peters	RP0200	18.75		●	●	●				
10	Richard Peters	RP2971	19.99		●	●	●	●			
11	Daniels	D131	21.75		●	●	●				
12	Rosena	RO25	22.50		●	●	●	●			
13	Richard Peters	RP2810	26.50		●	●	●	●			
14	Daniels	D132	26.75		●	●	●	●			
15	Terry Falcon	TF14	26.75		●	●	●				
16	Richard Peters	RP2930	27.50		●	●	●	●			
17	Rosena	RO82	28.50		●	●	●	●			
18	Rosena	RO32	28.50		●	●	●	●			
19	Rosena	RO22	28.99		●	●	●	●			
20	Daniels	D121	29.25		●	●	●	●			●
21	Richard Peters	RP2399	29.50		●	●	●	●		●	
22	Richard Peters	RP2142	29.50		●	●	●	●		●	
23	Daniels	D332	29.50		●	●	●	●			
24	Terry Falcon	TF18	29.50		●	●	●	●			
25	Terry Falcon	TF69	32.25		●	●	●				
26	Rosena	RO43	32.50		●	●	●	●			
27	Richard Peters	RP1556	34.50		●	●	●	●			
28	Rosena	RO31	34.50		●	●	●	●			
29	Luminex	LM651	35.50		●	●	●	●			●
30	Terry Falcon	TF70	36.25		●	●	●	●			
31	Daniels	D424	36.50		●	●	●	●			
32	Terry Falcon	TF67	39.99		●	●	●		●		
33	Rosena	RO30	42.99		●	●	●	●			
34	Browning	B51-3	44.50			●		●			
35	Daniels	D515	44.50		●		●	●			
36	Terry Falcon	TF93	44.50		●	●	●		●		
37	Rosena	RO62	48.50		●	●	●	●			
38	Terry Falcon	TF20	54.50		●	●	●		●		
39	Terry Falcon	TF45	69.50			●	●		●		
40	Terry Falcon	TF84	99.00		●	●	●	●			

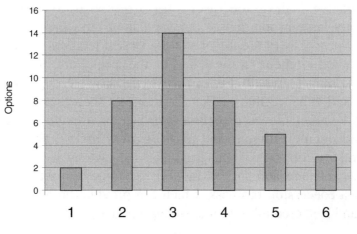

There will always be some key factors, which can be weighed up fairly objectively:

- *Price assortment*

  How many models should there be in each price band? Some market information would be helpful in answering this question.

  Where is the strongest consumer demand? The most popular price bands can support greater product variety. Too wide an assortment in the less popular price bands would be undesirable and depress the overall rate of stockturn. The price profile of the range will normally form a curve referred to as a normal distribution. (See the bar chart on page 49)

- *Brand*

  Brand is more important in some product categories than others. The questions the buyer has to address will include things like:

  - What brands will our customers expect to find in store?
  - Which brands, if included in the range, will lend credibility to the range as a whole?

  Conversely, which brand names, if absent from the range, would weaken the overall product offer? From the buyer's perspective, the buying terms agreed with each supplier will influence the buyer's judgement in deciding between Brand X and Brand Y where the product selling features themselves are reasonably comparable.

In this example, the range of irons has been reduced by more than 50% to provide a tighter, more focused assortment. (See 'Rationalised Irons Range' opposite.) Buying policy will influence brand assortment, price assortment and the width of range.

From a broader perspective, buying policy will determine which product areas the retailer will trade in. There are retailers who have gained a reputation for excellence in certain product areas. For example, a significantly large proportion of the population buys their underwear from Marks & Spencer. MFI are the one of the largest retailers of flat-packed and pre-assembled kitchens in the UK. For these retailers, these are areas of traditional product strength. Policy on merchandise assortment would seek to maintain and enhance that market position. At the other end of the scale, there will be retailers who recognise their lack of strength in certain product areas, and decide either to try to strengthen their market position, or alternatively, to opt out of that product area, leaving it to others who are already established and successful. For example, department stores may introduce a concession business, which can provide the necessary specialist strength and lend credibility to the overall product offer.

Rationalised Irons Range

Ref No	Brand	Product	Selling Price	PRODUCT FEATURES							
				Travel Iron	Dry Iron	Steam	Spray	Jet of Steam	Boost of Steam	Coloured	Cordless
2	Janini	JR69	8.99	•	•	•					
5	Janini	JR48	12.75		•	•	•	•			
8	Daniels	D220	17.99		•	•	•				
10	Richard Peters	RP2971	19.99		•	•	•	•			
12	Rosena	RO25	22.50		•	•	•	•			
13	Richard Peters	RP2810	26.50		•	•	•	•			
17	Rosena	RO82	28.50		•	•	•	•			
19	Rosena	RO22	28.99		•	•	•	•			
21	Richard Peters	RP2399	29.50		•	•	•	•		•	
22	Richard Peters	RP2142	29.50		•	•	•	•		•	
27	Richard Peters	RP1556	34.50		•	•	•	•			
29	Luminex	LM651	35.50		•	•	•	•			•
30	Terry Falcon	TF70	36.25		•	•	•	•			
32	Terry Falcon	TF67	39.99		•	•	•		•		
35	Daniels	D515	44.50		•	Excel Plus	•	•			
36	Terry Falcon	TF93	44.50		•	•	•		•		
37	Rosena	RO62	48.50		•	•	•	•	•		
38	Terry Falcon	TF20	54.50		•	•	•		•		
39	Terry Falcon	Tf45	69.50		Variable	•			•		

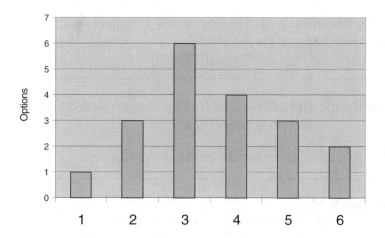

Clearance Policy

However good you think your range is, there will always be some need for product clearance! The customer will not always support the buyer's view that the product is *desirable*. This could be for any number of reasons – price, design, style, colour, size, etc. Suppliers will periodically discontinue products to make way for new product ideas. This will prompt the buyer to refresh their range assortment by deleting old products and adding new ones.

Whatever the reason for product deletion, what will happen to the stock? You could do several things with it:

- If it is seasonal product, it could be put away in a stockroom or warehouse until it becomes seasonal again next year – in other words, remove it from display. This will mean that stockholding will be inflated by an amount of "dead stock" for up to 12 months. Another point to consider is how well the product will "weather" over the storage period. Will it look as good as new when it is brought out again, or will the packaging (or the product itself) look old and battered?

- Support and co-operation could be sought from the supplier to take stock back, or, fund a markdown to help with the product or range clearance.
- The stock could be marked down and cleared. This will inevitably mean progressive markdown action until the product has cleared. The first price reduction, even if initially successful at clearing stock, will not usually be the last reduction. As the volume of reduced product sells, it becomes more difficult to sell. The assortment becomes poorer as the best selling options sell out, the product becomes more difficult to display as the quantity reduces and therefore it is less likely to attract customer attention. A deeper price cut is usually needed.

 In many businesses, markdowns equate to "failure" and are seen as an unwanted cost to the margin.

Assignment 3:5 Complete our Policy Issues Action Plan – Merchandise Policy

What is your company's policy on markdowns and clearance?

Policy Issues Action Plan

Merchandise Policy	What is your current policy? Is it formally written down, or just informally understood?	What actually happens now? Does practice comply with policy?	Action What needs to be done to bring practice into line with policy?
1 Width of Product Range Is the width of your product range guided or determined by policy?			
2. Clearance What is your clearance policy? What is your attitude to mark-downs?			

8. Summary

In this chapter, we have considered how various aspects of policy affect the relationships that buyers have with their suppliers, and the relationships that the company has with its customers and the wider community:

- the issues that are relevant and important to these groups
- the comparative benefits of broad and narrow supply bases
- policy on customer service including complaints policy along with its relevance to the buyer
- promotional policy with its potential for significantly enhancing or undermining buying performance.

Central to the buying role, we have looked at:

- the influence buying policy brings to bear on product range planning through its policies relating to merchandise assortment.

To use a board game analogy – buying policy sets out the rules of the game. If the buyers are the players, and the game board is the retail market in which they operate, where is the toy money that will allow them to play? And how much will they be allowed to play with?

In the real life situation, this will be the Open to Buy as defined within the buying budget! It will show what amount of money is available for investment in stock and when. It will allow the buyer to "enter the game".

Our next chapter looks at planning the budget and creating the financial framework that will guide and limit the buyer's spending.

Checklist

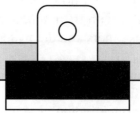

1. *The emphasis today is on establishing working partnerships with suppliers, sharing management information and working together in areas of common interest, such as stock delivery, distribution, promotional activity and in-store availability.*

2. *A standard "terms of supply" contract drawn up by the retailer is quite common. It can make life easier for the buyer at the initial negotiation stage.*

3. *A good supplier relationship is one that is effective for both parties. In other words, a good supplier relationship is one that works!*

4. *Whatever the company policy, remember that as a buyer, your reputation goes with you from job to job. When you are offered a gift, always ask yourself what motivates the supplier to make the offer and what might motivate you to accept?*

5. *The ethical stance taken by the retailer, and reflected in its Buying Policy, will influence and guide the buyer's product sourcing, ranging and buying decisions.*

6. *If a retailer wants to change its customer profile, it may have to change its name, its image, its level of customer service, its product range, or all of these things!*

7. *It can prove very costly to resolve some customer complaints. However, it can prove even more costly to fail to resolve the complaint.*

8. *Planned promotional activity can be built into the buying plan. But, unplanned promotional activity can create problems for the buyer.*

9. *Compliance with the letter of the law does not automatically mean compliance with the spirit of it!*

10. *More product options don't always mean more choice!*

11. *In many businesses, markdowns equate to "failure" and are seen as an unwanted cost to the margin.*

PART TWO

THE BUYING PROCESS

"The more rapidly trends change in your merchandise, the more disciplined your approach needs to be. Buyers need to be very clear about the changing strengths and weaknesses in their assortment."

Carole Lee
Director of Buying – Fashion Accessories
John Lewis Partnership

4

Planning the Budget

1. Introduction

In this chapter we are going to look at the buying budget and its relationship to the overall financial budget for the business. We will examine each component part of the buying budget: sales, stock, margin, markdowns and open to buy, working through the planning process step by step. Open to buy is created as a result of sales, stock and markdown planning and is an important budgetary element that needs to be fully understood. Here, we define it and look at the factors that affect it so that we can understand how to truly manage the spend.

 Every buyer should be fully aware of the individual budgetary elements of sales, stock, margin, markdowns and open to buy and understand how they interact within the budget.

Every business has an overall financial budget which defines its plans for:

- sales
- operating stock levels
- gross and net profit
- costs.

The buying budget fits within this budgetary plan.

Why Do We Need It?

From the broad company perspective, the buying budget impacts on cash flow. Cash flow is the term used to describe the movement of money into, and out of, a business. In retailing, on the incoming side of the equation is the cash received from customers for goods sold and, on the outgoing side it is the money paid for goods (or services) to suppliers. The buying budget predicts sales and defines the required expenditure on stock.

From a buying perspective, the buying budget provides a financial framework which allows management to control the spend, the stocks and manage the margin through markdowns.

 The buying budget provides a set of targets against which actual performance can be measured.

2. Planning

Whereas the financial budget is prepared for a financial year, the *buying budget* may cover either a full year or just a selling season (typically a half year). Seasonal buying budgets are particularly relevant to highly seasonal areas of business, e.g. clothing.

The first step in the buying process *should be* the planning of the budget. However, in real life it is very often the case that some or all of the season's buying is done before the financial planning is complete!

What would *you* do in the absence of a buying budget?

A common solution is to use last year's plan for the same season. Since it is likely that sales will be higher this year than last, the open to buy produced by this method is likely to be understated and, for obvious reasons, this is preferable to an overstated or exaggerated open to buy.

How is a buying budget put together? Who makes the decisions?

You may have come across the expressions "top down" and "bottom up". A "top down" budget is one where the figures are decided at a senior level within the business and are given to the buyers to achieve. A "bottom up" budget is one where, not surprisingly, the reverse is the case – the buyers in the business construct the budget by determining the budgets for their individual responsibility areas. These individual plans are then "rolled up" to give a total budget for the business.

A totally top down budget would be dictatorial and probably impractical; a totally bottom up budget could fail to meet company objectives for gross profit! The budget usually results from a combination of both methods, and might typically be constructed in this way:

Senior management would be aware of the overheads of the business and how much gross profit needs to be generated to cover those costs to provide a pre-determined, residual net profit. Using the top down method, they might then determine a "top level" plan for sales, stocks and gross profit. In a department store business for example, the budget might be defined down to department level so that the considerations of product and margin mix can be taken into account.

The buying department might then be given that top line data to break down into product sections and then to produce a phased plan.

3. The Process

So what of the process itself? Where should we start?

Some elements of the budget need to be complete before others can be started. For example, you need to have determined the sales plan for the whole planning period before you can look at phasing the sales by week and/or by month.

The Planning Pyramid illustrates one method of approach. It provides a logical, step by step planning sequence, which builds up the budget in layers.

The Planning Pyramid

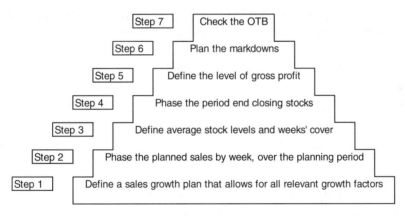

We will follow the 7 steps in our analysis of the planning process.

Following a planning sequence such as this should avoid a lot of re-working of the figures that could result from a less structured approach.

Get the plans "signed off" by senior management at each stage before proceeding to the next so that you can avoid having to revise figures over and over again!

4. Sales Growth

Defining a Sales Growth Plan

How do you assess the potential for sales growth?

Case History

Two senior managers of a multi-national corporation were overheard on a flight from London to New York:

"We really should put some plans in place for next year's budget. I think we should go for 10% sales growth."

"O.K., Jim, I'll put the wheels in motion and plan around that figure."

That, believe it or not, was the beginning of the planning process!

A "finger in the air" approach to planning sales growth is not uncommon, and could produce a result that proves achievable and accurate in hindsight! On the other hand it might not. It is certainly a high-risk strategy.

 A structured approach that identifies and evaluates each assumption on sales growth is probably safer than an inspired guess!

So, how should we define our sales growth rate?

If we were planning our buying budget for the Spring season we would take actual sales for the Spring season of the previous year as a base. Starting from this base, we need to consider every factor that could provide sales growth. Here are some possibilities:

- *Price inflation*
  By what percentage do we expect sales to grow year on year due to price inflation? If you are buying branded products, where there are Recommended Retail Prices (RRPs) that are largely observed by the retail trade, what those suppliers decide to do with their pricing will be of great significance to your sales growth rate. If your business is non-branded and you fix your own price levels, you may wish to consult government statistics for inflation and use them in your planning. If your business has a mixture of these two types of product, then, logically, you would choose a growth percentage that takes both factors into account.

- *Opening a new store or section within a department*
  Branching out into a new product area would provide incremental growth, or, in other words, additional business which should be quantified and then expressed as a rate of growth on our sales base.

- *Closing a store or section within a department*
  The same applies to store or section closures as openings – but in reverse! The growth rate in this case would be a negative value.

- *Refurbishment*
  If a refurbishment or renovation of the whole or part of the store or department is planned, then the event would be expected to affect sales. The effect may be a negative one whilst some of the more disruptive building work is carried out, followed by a positive and beneficial effect on sales on completion of the refurbishment. Again, this impact needs to be quantified so that it can be reflected in the sales budget.

- *"Like-for-Like" growth*
  This refers to the organic growth you expect as a result of general improvement to your business operation, e.g. improved marketing, increased advertising activity, improved customer service through administrative, procedural or sales training initiatives for staff.

 Avoid the natural tendency to be over optimistic when assessing like-for-like sales growth potential.

Assignment 4:1 Planning sales growth

Use the sample format shown below to create a sales plan for next year, or next season.

1. Take a look at your current year or half year's actual sales performance.
2. Forecast sales to the end of the period.
3. Construct a sales plan for next year or season.
4. Review the result with your manager, discussing the assumptions you have made for each growth factor: price inflation, store/dept/section openings and closures, expansion or contraction, re-furbishment.

Planning Sales Growth

			Growth Factors					
Textiles department	This year Sales Plan	% inc TY v LY	Like-for-like growth		New Stores	Store Closures	Store Re-fits	Last year Sales
			%	£				
Bed Linen	10,565	15.64	5.60	512	1,171	(457)	203	9,136
Quilts and Pillows	3,154	11.65	4.40	124	289	(141)	57	2,825
Ready Made Curtains	5,492	-2.51	(10.70)	(603)	561	(282)	182	5,633
Made-to-measure Curtains	2,278	-18.72	(28.60)	(801)	344	(140)	73	2,803
Nets	1,120	7.18	2.80	29	79	(52)	19	1,045
Tracks, Poles & Accessories	934	19.87	5.10	40	134	(39)	20	779
Blinds	594	19.27	5.60	28	86	(25)	7	498
Household Linen	1,262	13.79	4.00	44	127	(55)	37	1,109
Bathroom Textiles	3,365	9.46	3.50	108	282	(154)	55	3,074
Cushions	1,201	9.61	3.40	37	93	(55)	30	1,096
TOTAL	29,964	7.03	-1.72	(482)	3,166	(1,400)	683	27,997

5. Sales Phasing

Having arrived at a total sales volume to be achieved within the planning period, the next step is to phase the sales by week. What sales pattern will you use to spread your planned sales?

It may be appropriate to phase your sales as last year with some amendments to allow for:

- changes in the promotional calendar
- movement of public holidays such as Easter
- new section/department/store openings
- section/department /store closures
- section/department/store refurbishment.

Having done this, it is helpful to review the resultant sales pattern critically and consider the planned year on year sales growth by week, or by trading period, to ensure that the plan looks sensible (i.e. conduct a "reality check').

Probably the two most helpful methods of reviewing your phased sales plans are:

1. This year vs. last year (see "Sales Phasing Review" below).
2. A sales line graph, which will illustrate the pattern created by the individual weekly planned sales volumes (see "Sales Line Graph" below).

Sales Phasing Review

	Period1			Period 2			Period 3			Period 4		
	TY	LY	% var	TY	LY	% var	TY	LY	% var	TY	LY	% var
Menswear	87,423	82,321	6.2	86,232	74,121	16.3	77,241	67,568	14.3	95,467	85,586	11.5

	Period 5			Period 6			Period 7		
	TY	LY	% var	TY	LY	% var	TY	LY	% var
Menswear	80,158	77.766	3.1	94,821	81,762	16	521,343	469,124	11.1

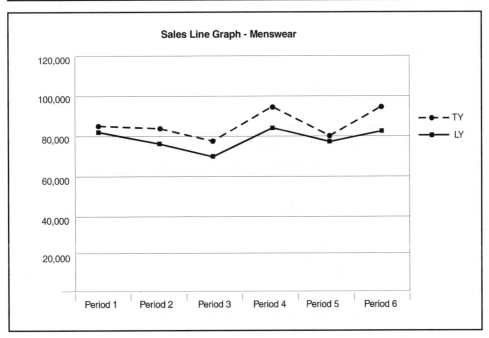

Sales Line Graph - Menswear

Company policy will determine how promotional the business will be. It may be that the promotions schedule is provisionally put in place to support the sales pattern demonstrated by last year's sales. Scheduled promotions may be fairly general to the business as a whole, e.g. Summer Sale, Mid-Season Sale, Easter Promotion. In this case the buyers may review the planned promotions and add some further promotional activity specific to their product area.

Planned promotional activity needs to be taken into account when phasing planned sales, since it *can* and *should* distort the sales pattern!

 Promotions can make a significant impact on your planned sales phasing.

Assignment 4:2 Use the planned sales figure generated in the previous assignment to create a phased sales plan.

Ask your manager to review it with you and assess its credibility.

---

6. Stockturn

What is stockturn?

 In retailing, we invest money in stock and aim to turn it back into cash as quickly as possible. The number of times we can do this within a planning period is our rate of stockturn.

Mathematically, $\text{Stockturn} = \dfrac{\text{Sales}}{\text{Average Stock}}$

Note: Both sales and stock in this calculation must be expressed in the same way, i.e. they must both be at either cost or selling value and either exclude or include VAT.

If we have sales of £10,000 and an annual rate of stockturn of 5 then our average stock would be £2,000.

We can utilise the stockturn formula to find any one missing value.

Example

Q. Given sales of £11,000 and an annual stockturn rate of 3.71, what would be the average stock value?

A. The average stock value would be £2964.96 (£11,000 divided by 3.71)

Average stock can be expressed simply as a money value. However it is often described as representative of a number of weeks sales cover.

Example

Planned sales	Average stock	Stockturn	Weeks cover
£25,000	£5769.23	4.33	12.00 (i.e. 52 divided by 4.33)

 Stockturn is the measure of stock productivity and is very often a fixed, non-negotiable element within the buying budget!

How hard your stock is required to work to produce a specified level of sales will usually be determined for you, i.e. top down. However, the rate of stockturn, when applied to planned sales produces an average stock value which will allow some flexibility in the phasing of individual closing stocks within the planning period as long as the required average is maintained.

7. Stock Phasing

Having defined a planned average stock we now have to define a suitable pattern of closing stocks for each week or period end. One way of phasing the closing stocks would be to apply the average value throughout the planning period. This is often a good starting point for the phasing process. However, the plan at this stage will probably have some unacceptable weaknesses.

- The closing stock at the end of the first period may show a level which represents a sharp variance from the planned or forecast closing stock at the end of the prior planning period.
- The open to buy created by such a phasing may be far from ideal!

Stock Phasing Data

Textiles

Retail incl VAT £k	Pd 1	Pd 2	Pd 3	Pd 4	Pd 5	Pd 6	Pd 6	Pd 8	Pd 9	Pd 10	Pd 11	Pd 12	Pd 13	Total
Opening stock	450	260	80	-108	-269	-473	-726	-870	-1196	-1515	-1873	-2223	-2718	
Planned sales	219	171	181	161	192	225	176	294	263	302	287	480	376	3327
Markdowns	-29	9	7	0	12	28	-32	32	56	56	63	15	105	322
Closing stock	260	80	-108	-269	-473	-726	-870	-1196	-1515	-1873	-2223	-2718	-3199	
Planned closing stock	771	771	771	771	771	771	771	771	771	771	771	771	771	
Planned weeks cover	17.1	16.2	16.4	14.6	13.0	12.4	10.6	10.7	10.5	8.0	7.1	10.1	11.9	
Open to buy	511	180	188	161	204	253	144	326	319	358	350	495	481	3970

Planned sales P1 - P13:	£3,327k
Average stock P1 - P13:	£771k
Rate of stockturn:	4.32
No of weeks cover	12.0

Notes
1. The average stock has been applied to each period end as the planned closing stock, giving a flat phasing pattern
2. This has produced a relatively large amount of OTB at the beginning and end of the year (see Periods 1, 12 and 13)

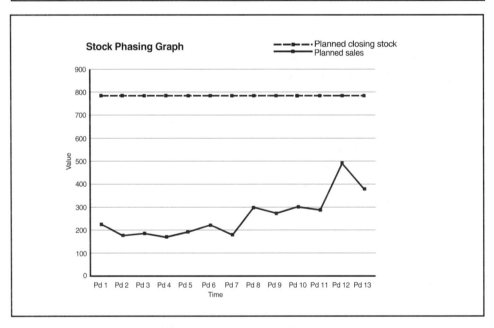

Another possible starting point is to copy last year's pattern of closing stocks, but this also has its dangers. For example – was last year's phasing so perfect that it should be used as a template for this year?

Let's consider for a moment the relationship between sales and stock. Stock will normally have to be bought in advance of sales. Therefore the sales pattern will mirror the stock pattern, with a time lag to allow adequate processing time between goods received and the establishment of a shop floor display.

We might amend the stock phasing to look something like this:

Revised Stock Phasing Data

Textiles

Retail incl VAT £k	Pd 1	Pd 2	Pd 3	Pd 4	Pd 5	Pd 6	Pd 6	Pd 8	Pd 9	Pd 10	Pd 11	Pd 12	Pd 13	Total
Opening stock	450	260	80	-108	-269	-473	-726	-870	-1196	-1515	-1873	-2223	-2718	
Planned sales	219	171	181	161	192	225	176	294	263	302	287	480	376	3327
Markdowns	-29	9	7	0	12	28	-32	32	56	56	63	15	105	322
Closing stock	260	80	-108	-269	-473	-726	-870	-1196	-1515	-1873	-2223	-2718	-3199	
Planned closing stock	509	534	604	615	715	763	844	760	1010	1143	1086	798	644	
Planned weeks cover	10.9	12.0	12.6	12.3	12.3	12.4	11.8	10.7	11.5	12	11.5	10.4	9.8	
Open to buy	249	205	258	172	304	301	225	242	569	491	293	207	327	3843

Planned sales P1 - P13:	£3,327k
Average stock P1 - P13:	£771k
Rate of stockturn:	4.32
No of weeks cover	12.0

Notes
1. The planned closing stock has been phased by period to produce an acceptable phasing of the OTB
2. In comparison to the first draft of the plan, where average stock was applied in a flat pattern,
    there is less OTB in periods 1, 12 and 13
    there is more OTB in Periods 9 and 10 to allow for the intake of new season's stock

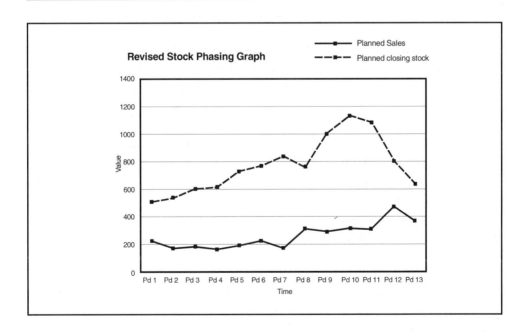

8. Planned Margin

This is simply the difference between the cost and the selling price expressed as a percentage of the selling price. It is the margin on the goods at the time they are bought, the margin you *plan* to make. Whilst the method of calculating margin varies from company to company, the principles remain the same. Some will quote an entirely VAT free margin, as in example 1, whilst others will mix VAT inclusive and VAT exclusive values, as illustrated in example 2.

Examples

Selling price	£10.00
VAT exclusive selling price	£ 8.51
Cost price	£ 5.00
Gross profit	£ 3.51

1. The margin is 41.24%, i.e. £3.51 expressed as a percentage of £8.51

2. The margin is 35.1%, i.e. £3.51 expressed as a percentage of £10.00

Simplistically, we should aim for the highest possible planned margin. We are, however, constrained on the one hand by the cost price (the result of supplier negotiation), and on the other, by the selling price which is governed by what is commercially viable. These are the two parameters that define the planned margin.

Our planned margin is the potential profit we stand to make if we sell our goods at full price. A nice thought! However, in reality there will be an element of markdowns applied to those original selling prices before they translate into actual sales and generate gross profit.

Where the sales and markdown plans and achieved margin targets are known, the planned margin is automatically established. Where *any three* of these four factors (sales, planned margin, markdowns and achieved margin) are known, the fourth, missing factor can be calculated.

Within the product mix, there will be lines carrying planned margins which are both *higher than* and *lower than* the budget. The skill is in managing the mix to achieve the overall required rate. This will be covered in greater depth later in the book.

So, we know what margin we *plan* to make, but what do we expect to actually achieve?

9. Achieved Margin

The achieved margin may simply be the planned margin adjusted for markdowns. For our purposes here, we will accept this definition. However, achieved margin *may* also include supplier settlement discounts, retrospective rebates and other positive or negative factors. Achieved margin is almost always a budgetary factor which is determined *for* the buyer.

Achieved margin is the expression of gross profit as a percentage of sales.

Example

Sales £5,000   Gross Profit £2,000   Achieved Margin 40%

There will always be high and low margin lines relative to the budget.

As stated in the previous section on planned margin, the buyer's skill in managing the mix is critically important if the overall achieved margin target is to be reached.

10. Gross Profit

Gross profit is the difference between the cost price and the selling price after the deduction of markdowns. It is the profit realised when the goods are actually sold and it is expressed as a value. In some retail organisations, the gross profit figure may include other factors like settlement discount that enhance gross profit, and factors like shrinkage, which reduce gross profit. But, for our purposes here, we will accept the first definition.

 Businesses need to make a profit to ensure they stay in business! The buyer's role in this is critically important – they are the " profit generators."

11. Markdowns

There are two kinds of markdown – promotional and clearance. Promotional markdowns, assuming they are planned sufficiently in advance, can often be costed into the planned margin and have no negative impact on the realised gross profit. (A lower buying price may be agreed with the supplier which would offset the reduction in selling price, thereby leaving the achieved margin intact.)

Clearance markdowns however, are different. They are a measure of how successful or unsuccessful the buyer has been at selecting product which the customer finds desirable at the price that the buyer has set.

In terms of the mechanics of planning markdowns within the Buying Budget, markdowns are applied to *reduce* the selling price of goods. They thereby reduce the selling value of the stock held. Markdowns have an adverse effect on gross profit.

Conversely, markups *increase* the selling price of goods, make a positive impact on gross profit and *increase* the selling value of the stock held. Since markdowns usually exceed markups within any given planning period, we will refer only to markdowns, and think of them as net markdowns, i.e. after deduction of any markups.

Within the buying budget, the required level of sales and achieved margin are generally fixed and this determines the amount of gross profit to be achieved. A realistic markdown value can usually be estimated. The combination of these three factors: sales, achieved margin and markdowns will define the planned margin, which can then be calculated. Alternatively, the sales, planned margin and achieved margin may be fixed. In this case, the level of markdowns are defined and can be calculated. The inter-relationship of sales, planned margin, achieved margin and markdowns is illustrated in the "Sales, Margin and Markdowns" diagram. In this illustration, the sales, planned margin and achieved margin have been taken from the buying budget, which means that the value of markdowns are automatically defined and have been calculated.

Sales, Margin and Markdowns

Gross Sales (incl VAT)	Gross Sales (excl VAT)	Cost of Sales	Planned Sales (excl VAT)	Planned Sales (inc VAT)	Planned Margin %	Planned Margin £	Achieved Margin %	Gross Profit	Planned Markdown
3,744	3,186	1,434	**2,607**	3,063	55.0	1,752	45.0	1,173	681
Ex VAT Gross Sales plus VAT at 17.5%	Cost of sales divided by the reciprocal of the Planned Margin %	Ex VAT planned sales minus the Gross Profit value	**Buying Budget**	Ex VAT Sales plus VAT at 17.5%	**Buying Budget**	Gross Sales (ex VAT) multiplied by the Planned Margin %	**Buying Budget**	Planned ex VAT Sales multiplied by Achieved Margin	The difference between Gross Sales and Planned Sales (inc VAT)
3,186 + VAT	1,434 divided by 45.0% (100-55)	2,607-1,173		2,607 + VAT		3,186 x 55%		2,607 x 45%	3,744 - 3,063

Notes

Gross Sales are *theoretical* sales ie, *before* markdowns

The figures printed in **bold type** represent values that are fixed, taken from the buying budget. All other values are calculated as shown.

All other values are calculated, as shown. Margins are exclusive of VAT

How much markdown allowance should be built into the buying budget?

Promotional policy will indicate whether the promotional element of the total markdown value will be less than, greater than or the same as last year as a percentage of sales. Whilst some allowance may be made within the buying budget for clearance markdowns, this will often be an area where year-on-year reduction is sought in the drive for improved buying efficiency.

Once the markdown plan has been established, it has to be phased. How should we spread our total planned markdown value?

The promotional calendar will probably have the most significant impact on the phasing of promotional markdowns. A good starting point for markdown phasing would be to use the pattern of markdowns demonstrated by actual markdowns last year, if the planned promotional activity followed the same pattern. However, changes in the promotional calendar, year-on-year, should prompt a review and possibly some amendment of the markdown phasing.

The timing of clearance markdowns (if they are built into the buying budget) should take full account of seasonal stock clearance dates. For example, when should a seasonal product like swimwear or Christmas decorations be reduced and cleared?

Assignment 4:3 *Take last year's sales and promotional markdowns and assess what percentage of total sales those markdowns represented.*

Now decide how to phase the markdown spend by reviewing your planned promotional activity compared to that of last year.

---

12. Open to buy

Open to buy is often simply referred to as OTB. What is it?

Open to buy is the amount of money available to the buyer to spend on stock in any given period. We can use a simple example to illustrate the concept:

Example

Imagine you are opening your own shop. You will obviously need stock to sell. Let's assume you open your shop with £50,000 of stock at retail value.

In the first 4 weeks of trading, you achieve sales of £20,000 and incur markdowns totalling £1,200. If you planned to close that first trading period with the same amount of stock as you started with, you would need an open to buy of £21,200 to replace your sales and end with your required stock value.

Open to buy is the result, arithmetically, of deducting sales and markdowns from the opening stock and taking that figure away from a planned closing stock. It is generally, although not always expressed at *selling value*.

Sample Open to buy

Retail inc VAT £k	Pd 1	Pd 2	Pd 3	Pd 4	Pd 5	Pd 6
Opening stock	450	231	51	-137	-298	-502
Planned sales	219	171	181	161	192	225
Markdowns	0	9	7	0	12	28
Closing stock	231	51	-137	-298	-502	-763
Planned closing stock	450	548	617	614	735	785
Open to buy	219	278	257	158	325	303

Open to buy expressed as a formula looks like this:

OTB = Planned closing stock – (Opening stock, less sales + markdowns)

In the "opening your own shop" example above, the sum would look like this:

OTB = £50,000 – (£50,000 – £21,200) = £50,000 – £28,800 = £21,200

It is easy to see that, where the planned opening and planned closing stocks for a period are of equal value, the open to buy will be equal to the planned sales and markdowns for that period.

Open to buy is an element of the budget that is not so much planned as created as a result of planning sales, stocks and markdowns.

The open to buy created in the first draft of the phased budget may not be available in the right periods to accommodate the buyer's spending plans. Remember that stock needs to be in place *in advance of* sales. We should be able to model the open to buy to provide a more suitable plan. The means of doing this is through the manipulation of the closing stocks.

Here are a few laws of "cause and effect" as applied to open to buy. *In the current period:*

- a higher planned closing stock will create *more OTB*
- a lower planned closing stock will create *less OTB*.

However, *in the next period*:

- a higher planned closing stock in the previous period will become a higher opening stock in the next, creating **less OTB** there
- a lower planned closing stock in the previous period will become a lower opening stock in the next, creating **more OTB** there.

Changing the Open to Buy

Before adjustment to Period 1 Planned Closing Stock

Retail inc VAT £k	Pd 2	Pd 2	Pd 3	Pd 4	Pd 5	Pd 6	Total
Opening Stock	450	231	51	-137	-298	-502	
Planned Sales	219	171	181	161	192	225	1149
Markdowns	0	9	7	0	12	28	56
Closing Stock	231	51	-137	-298	-502	-763	
Planned Closing Stock	450	548	617	614	735	785	
Under Stock	219	497	754	912	1237	1548	1548
Open to Buy	219	278	257	158	325	311	1548

After increasing Period 1 Planned Closing Stock

Retail inc VAT £k	Pd 2	Pd 2	Pd 3	Pd 4	Pd 5	Pd 6	Total
Opening Stock	450	231	51	-137	-298	-502	
Planned Sales	219	171	181	161	192	225	1149
Markdowns	0	9	7	0	12	28	56
Closing Stock	231	51	-137	-298	-502	-763	
Planned Closing Stock	500	548	617	614	735	785	
Under Stock	269	497	754	912	1237	1548	1548
Open to Buy	269	228	257	158	325	311	1548

Manipulating closing stocks to provide adequate amounts of open to buy in the right place is often a trial and error process, where the cycle of amending, reviewing and amending again is frequently repeated to get the best result.

13. Summary

We have examined each component part of the buying budget: sales, stocks, gross profit and open to buy, and worked through the planning process. We have also looked at how the open to buy can be manipulated by the amendment of planned closing stocks to provide the best possible pattern of expenditure that will support the achievement of our sales plan.

Now that we have our open to buy, how shall we spend it?

What we need is a shopping list!

Chapter 5 deals with how to formulate just such a "shopping list", more properly referred to as a Range Structure Plan.

Checklist

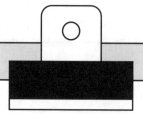

1. *Every buyer should be fully aware of the individual budgetary elements of sales, stock, margin, markdowns and open to buy and understand how they interact within the budget.*

2. *The buying budget provides a set of targets against which actual performance can be measured.*

3. *Get the plans "signed off" by senior management at each stage before proceeding to the next so that you can avoid having to revise figures over and over again!*

4. *A structured approach that identifies and evaluates each assumption on sales growth is probably safer than an inspired guess!*

5. *Avoid the natural tendency to be over optimistic when assessing like- for- like sales growth potential.*

6. *Promotions can make a significant impact on the planned sales pattern.*

7. *In retailing, we invest money in stock and aim to turn it back into cash as quickly as possible. The number of times we can do this within a planning period is our rate of stockturn.*

8. *Stockturn is the measure of stock productivity and is very often a fixed, non-negotiable element within the buying budget!*

9. *Businesses need to make a profit to ensure they stay in business! The buyers play a critically important role in this – they are the "profit generators."*

10. *Open to buy is an element of the budget that is not so much planned, as created as a result of planning sales, stocks and markdowns.*

11. *Manipulating closing stocks to provide adequate amounts of open to buy in the right place is often a trial and error process, where the cycle of amending, reviewing and amending again is frequently repeated to get the best result.*

5

Range Structure Planning

1. Introduction

The Range Structure Plan combines the financial requirements of the business, as defined in the buying budget, with some of the core elements of buying strategy. The range structure plan creates a model for the merchandise range. This model is multi-dimensional, as we shall see, and provides guidance for the buyer in product selection and range building.

 The range structure plan combines budgetary and strategic criteria to create a shopping list for the buyer!

Why should we have a range structure plan to buy to? Why not just select the products and order them?

The main attraction of range structure planning is that it relates directly to the buying budget. Adherence to the range structure plan should ensure that the selected range and subsequent stock commitment is reasonably well balanced, and that the open to buy will not "run out" before some important, core part of the range has been bought. It also means that the end result – the selected range, as defined in the range plan, will conform to the originally defined targets, both financial, and strategic.

In this chapter we will examine range structure planning in some detail. We will:

- consider where range structure planning fits into the buying cycle
- consider the scope of the range structure plan
- review the process step by step, showing what the end results can look like, using some sample formats.

2. The Buying Cycle

Let's examine the series of events that lead up to the start of the trading season, and see where range structure planning fits into the buying cycle:

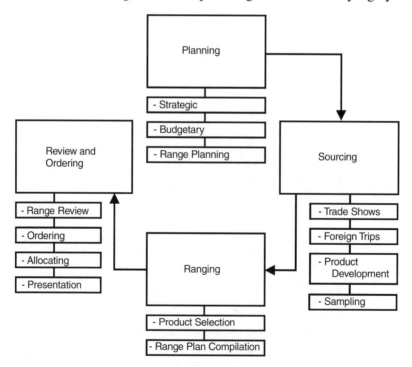

Whilst the timing and duration of each stage in the process will vary according to the product area and type of business, the sequence of events should be fairly consistent as illustrated in the sample Buying Schedule opposite.

Planning

The first step in the buying cycle, conducted at senior management level, will be the definition of the buying strategy. Budgetary planning will also start at this level, but as we have seen in our earlier chapter on the subject, the final budget is usually a mixture of top down and bottom up planning. These are the two pre-requisites for range structure planning where budgetary and strategic elements are brought together.

 Range structure planning should take place before stock commitments are made.

After all, what's the point in making a shopping list after you've done the shopping? Perhaps to see what you have forgotten? It may, of course, be too late then to do much about it, especially if you have spent all your money on other, non-essential products!

Sourcing

The next major stage in the process is sourcing the product. The buyer will visit trade shows to look at trends and new products. The buyer may also make visits abroad to look at retail stores in other countries where future market trends may be evident. This is particularly relevant in the clothing market where, for instance Paris, New York and Milan are considered important venues for buyers looking at fashion trends. There will also be visits to new and current suppliers. Where new products are being created and development is required, initial product selection will take place when the development work has been completed. Product selection may also be made from suppliers' existing branded or non-branded ranges. This will usually involve a certain amount of sampling to enable the buyer to compare and contrast product alternatives.

Buying Schedule

Department: _____ Year: _____ Season: _____

ACTIVITY	WEEK NUMBER																																																			
---	1	2	3	4	5	6	7	8	9	10	11	12	13	14	15	16	17	18	19	20	21	22	23	24	25	26	27	28	29	30	31	32	33	34	35	36	37	38	39	40	41	42	43	44	45	46	47	48	49	50	51	52
Planning																																																				
Strategic planning	▓																																																			
Budgetary planning			▓	▓																																																
Range structure planning					▓	▓																																													
Sourcing																																																				
Trade shows/Trips				▓		▓	▓																																													
Supplier visits									▓	▓	▓	▓	▓																																							
Initial product selection and sampling									▓	▓	▓					▓																																				
Range planning																																																				
Selection																▓	▓																																			
Range plan compilation																		▓	▓																																	
Review and ordering																																																				
Range review																			▓	▓																																
Ordering and allocation																					▓	▓																														
Range presentation																							▓	▓																												
"Sale"																										▓	▓	▓	▓	▓	▓																					
New season starts																																▓																				

Ranging

When the deadline for supplier submission of samples has been reached, the buyer makes the range selection, compiling a range plan to illustrate and define the range. The proposed range will then usually be reviewed by buying management before ordering and allocation of stock begins. Finally, before the season starts, the range will normally be presented to both buying and sales management in some format. This may take the form of a live presentation with product samples on show, or range details may simply be issued in some kind of range plan. Usually, presenting the range involves both these things!

The range plan will often be accompanied by layout plans showing the in-store location of each product. Further visual merchandising detail may be included defining how the product will be promoted.

3. Scope of the Plan

It is probably helpful at this point to draw a distinction between the range structure plan and the range plan.

 The range structure plan outlines the planned buy, whereas the range plan defines the actual buy.

Let's consider the scope of the range structure plan. What does it include?

Perhaps the best way to answer this question is to consider what will be of interest at the final range presentation when the buying cycle has been completed. What will management be looking for in that presentation? They will obviously be looking at the products themselves, but they will also be interested in the range structure:

- range profile
- range width
- average selling price
- margin mix
- sales density.

Range Profile

They will want to see that the range has the right merchandise mix in terms of price, style and customer appeal:

- price assortment: the "good, better, best" principle
- style assortment: contemporary, middle-of-the-road, or traditional
- customer appeal: in terms of age, socio-economic and lifestyle groups.

In the case of each of the three range profile aspects detailed above the management team will want to know:

- how many product options are in each category?
- what percentage of the total falls into each category?

Of the three aspects of merchandise mix, it is price assortment that is outlined within the range structure plan. (The two remaining factors: style assortment and customer appeal, form part of the range plan and are dealt with in Chapter 7 "Range Planning and Product Development").

Range Width

The reviewers will want to consider whether:

- the range is wide enough to offer the consumer real choice without causing confusion
- there is sufficient stock depth to mount a credible promotion of the product.

Average Selling Price

Another statistic that will be of interest is the average selling price. Any upward or downward price movement could be due to a conscious decision to move up or down market, or it could simply be the result of price inflation and the current market position may be maintained despite the increase.

Margin Mix

The overall margin mix will usually be of great interest as an indicator of the potential level of gross profit to be generated from the range dependent, of course, upon sales success. Higher risk product will normally be expected to carry a relatively high margin to offset any markdowns that may become necessary. Safer, core product may carry a lower margin but also a lower risk of sales failure.

Sales Density

The reviewers will want to consider:

- the expected sales per square foot (or metre) that will be generated
- whether that level of space productivity is acceptable – that is, does the anticipated sales (and gross profit) yield justify the space occupied?

If these are the main factors that will be of interest in the final range presentation, then all of these areas need to be covered within the range structure plan.

4. The Planning Process

Creating a range structure plan is rather like making a cake and, as with cake-making, what results is much more than just the sum of the separate ingredients.

The process involves the input of a number of budgetary and strategic assumptions which create other, new range criteria. The process can easily be illustrated as a series of inputs and outputs:

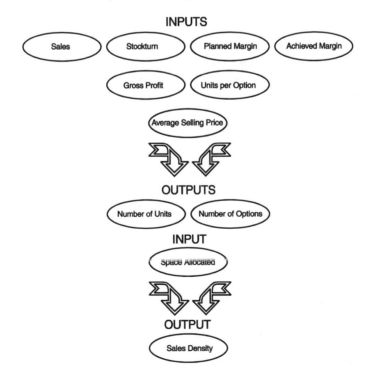

Let's examine these inputs and outputs a little more closely. Where do they come from? How are they defined?

A step by step review of the process reveals the answers.

5. Building the Plan

A range structure plan will normally cover a trading season, typically a half-year period.

The first step in the construction of our range structure plan, involves getting some background information to lay the foundations for the range structure. This should start with a review of trading history for the same season the previous year, to assess range efficiency in terms of:

- the percentage of product sold at full price compared to the amount of product bought
- the range width – did the range provide real choice or were there too many options? Would fewer options have resulted in better volume sales per option?
- the average selling price – was it too high or too low?

Answers to these questions involve fairly subjective judgement.

 Making decisions based on fact and applying best skill and judgement is what management in general, and buying in particular, is all about!

A good second step in preparation for the construction of our plan is a review of current trading performance. The review of trading performance last year for the season which is being planned, combined with a review of current trading performance, lays the foundation for range structure planning by forcing the following questions to be answered:

"How are we doing?"
"What have we learnt from recent experience relevant to the season being planned?"
"What should we do differently in the future?"
"What are we aiming for?"

Having laid the foundation, we can start building!

Stage 1 – Budgetary Plan

This first stage requires reference to the buying budget, which will have defined the following:

- the sales plan for the season
- the average stock value
- the planned and achieved margin requirements
- the gross profit.

When you have all of this information, you can proceed to the next stage of the plan. At each stage of the process, there are elements of the plan that have either been:

a) pre-defined, e.g. in the buying budget,
b) assumed by the buyer or buying manager, or
c) calculated from other input information.

So far, the information referred to comes under the category of "pre-defined" since it has been taken from the buying budget.

Stage 2 – Units and Options Plan

The creation of this stage of the plan will require two assumptions:

- the average selling price
- the average number of units per option.

Identification of these factors will allow the calculation of two further critical values:

- the total number of units – calculated by dividing the total stock value by the average selling price
- the total number of stock options – defined by dividing the total units by the assumed number of units per option.

This can be summarised as follows:

Example

	Pre-defined	Assumed	Calculated
Average selling price		£9.99	
Units per option		20	
Total stock value	£10,000		
No. of units			1001*
No. of options			50**

Note:

*1001 = £10,000 divided by £9.99

**50 = 1001 divided by 20

In certain circumstances, it may be more appropriate to change some of the assumed factors into calculated factors! For instance, instead of following the process shown above, you may want to assume a certain number of options and allow that assumption to drive out a stock depth per option (units per option) figure.

Example

On 60 options, the units per option would have to reduce to 16 (the number of units, 1001 divided by the number of options, 60) provided all the other factors remained constant.

Range width (as defined by the number of options), and range depth (as defined by the units per option), must conform to the total stock value requirement.

In practical terms, you can have a relatively wide range with little stock depth, or a relatively narrow range with a greater stock depth, but the combination of these two range parameters should conform to the stock value contained within the buying budget.

Stage 3 – Space Plan

Converting our units and options plan into a space plan will require the answers to a few more questions, such as how much space will one product option require for display?

This may be quite a complex question. Let's break this one down into three parts:

- Floor area (space)
- Fixturing
- Facings

Floor Area

Space in a shop or store may be measured in area: square feet or metres, or quoted as linear footage. A conversion factor can be applied to allow linear footage and sales floor area to be consolidated and quoted uniformly as area, or square footage.

Fixturing

What are the dimensions of the fixtures to be used, how much space do they occupy?

It may also be necessary to allow for non-selling areas within the store within the assessment of space occupied by certain types of fixture, e.g. escalators and customer walkways. It is this type of space, after all, that allows customer traffic access to the selling areas within the store.

Facings

The question to be answered here is what is the optimum number of options that should be displayed per facing?

We can illustrate this with a sample layout showing 30 facings of ladies gloves.

Layout Plan - Gloves

PVC Plain BLACK 2.99	PVC Plain BLACK 2.99	Knitted Plain BLACK 2.99	Knitted Plain Black 2.99	Leather imi-pec BLACK 19.99	Evening Glove BLACK 4.99
PVC Fancy BLACK 3.50	PVC Fancy BLACK 3.50	Knitted Fancy BLACK 2.99	Knitted Boucle BLACK 3.99	Leather imi-pec BLACK 19.99	Leather rayon BLACK 25.99
PVC Plain NAVY 2.99	PVC Plain NAVY 2.99	Knitted Plain NAVY 2.99	Knitted Fancy NAVY 2.99	Leather imi-pec NAVY 19.99	Leather rayon NAVY 25.99
PVC Fancy NAVY 3.50	PVC Fancy NAVY 3.50	Knitted Plain RED 2.99	Knitted Fancy RED 2.99	Leather imi-pec BROWN 19.99	Sheepskin Glove BROWN 19.99
PVC Plain BROWN 2.99	PVC Fancy BROWN 2.99	Knitted Plain BROWN 2.99	Knitted Plain CREAM 2.99	Sheepskin Mitt BROWN 9.99	Sheepskin Mitt BROWN 9.99

From our units and options plan we can see the total number of product options we want to accommodate. In this case there are 22 options:

- PVC plain in black, navy and brown
- PVC fancy in black, navy and brown
- knitted plain in black, navy, red, brown and cream
- knitted fancy in black and red
- knitted boucle in black
- leather imi-pec in black, navy and brown
- leather, rayon lined in black and navy
- sheepskin mitt in brown
- sheepskin glove in brown
- evening glove in black.

We can see that with 22 options and 30 display facings, there will be more than one facing per option. The display could be condensed to take up less space if required. The range could be displayed on 20 facings, if two of the options occupied the same facing.

Gloves Layout - Reduced Space

PVC Plain BLACK 2.99	Knitted Plain BLACK 2.99	Leather imi-pec BLACK 19.99	Leather rayon BLACK 25.99
PVC Fancy BLACK 3.50	Knitted Boucle BLACK 3.99	Leather imi-pec NAVY 19.99	Leather rayon NAVY 25.99
PVC Plain NAVY 2.99	Knitted Plain NAVY 2.99	Knitted Fancy RED and NAVY 2.99	Evening Glove BLACK 4.99
PVC Fancy NAVY 3.50	PVC Fancy BROWN 3.50	Knitted Plain RED 2.99	Leather imi-pec BROWN 19.99
PVC Plain BROWN 2.99	Knitted Plain CREAM & BROWN 2.99	Sheepskin Mitt BROWN 9.99	Sheepskin Glove BROWN 19.99

If we know what sort of fixtures will be used and what floor space those fixtures occupy, then we can assess the space that is required.

6. The Range Structure Plan

We have referred to the range structure plan simplistically as a shopping list for the buyer. It is, in reality, a very special kind of shopping list with many different dimensions … a multi-dimensional shopping list!

How can we best illustrate the various aspects of range structure?

There are many computer software packages available to help create and illustrate range structure plans but we will look at some sample format documentation here, which serves to illustrate the range parameters we have considered.

Let's take a look at some sample formats using our Autumn/Winter ladies glove range for illustration purposes.

Budgetary Plan

Budgetary Plan - Gloves												
Note:	1	2	3	4	5	6	7	8	9	10	11	12
	Sales			Planned Margin %	Achieved Margin %	Gross Profit £	Average Stock		Stockturn			
Autumn	Plan TY	Actual LY	+/- %				Plan TY	Actual LY	Last year		This year	
									Rate	Wks cover	Rate	Wks cover
Gloves	73,451	66,009	11.3	54.0	47.0	34,522	23,609	28,290	2.33	12.0	3.11	9.0

Notes:

1 This year's sales plan for the Autumn season (28 trading weeks)

2 Last year's actual sales for the same period

3 The rate of year-on-year sales growth

4 This year's Planned Margin rate

5 This year's planned rate of Achieved Margin (VAT inclusive calculation)

6 The budgeted Gross Profit. This is calculated by multiplying planned sales by the Achieved Margin rate.

7 The planned average stock is calculated by taking the sales plan, dividing it by the number of weeks (28) and multiplying the result by 9 (the planned rate of stockturn determines 9 weeks' cover.)

8 The actual average stock last year.

9 Last year's seasonal stockturn rate: £66,009 sales divided by £28,290 - the *actual* average stock.

10 Last year's weeks' cover: 28 weeks in the season divided by the stockturn rate of 2.33

11 This year's planned rate of stockturn as specified within the buying budget.

12 The planned rate of stockturn expressed as a number of weeks' cover, by taking the number of weeks in the season (28) and dividing by the stockturn rate of 3.11

You can see from the details here that the plan is to achieve sales of £73,451 at an achieved margin rate of 47% and thereby generate a gross profit of £34,522.

Units & Options Plan

By starting with the planned average stock taken from the budgetary plan and applying an assumed average selling price, the average stock in units can be calculated. Given an assumption about average units per option, the average number of options can be defined, as illustrated below:

Units and Options Plan - Gloves

Notes: Autumn	1 Planned Average Stock Value	2 Average Selling Price	3 No of Stores	4 Average Stock per Store (units)	5 Average Options per Store	6 Average Units per Option per Store
Gloves	23,609	6.71	8	440	21	21

Notes:

1 Taken from the budgetary plan
2 An assumed average selling price
3 The total number of stores ranged for Ladies' Gloves
4 The average stock value, divided first by the average selling price, and then by the number of stores
5 The average stock per store (in units) 440, divided by the assumed stock depth 21
6 An assumed stock depth

Space Plan

The space plan draws upon information contained in the Units and Options Plan i.e. the average number of options, and utilises the space requirement defined by the floor layout plan. When this information is combined with sales and gross profit figures, sales and gross profit per square foot can be calculated.

In our example the Floor Layout Plan might be as follows:

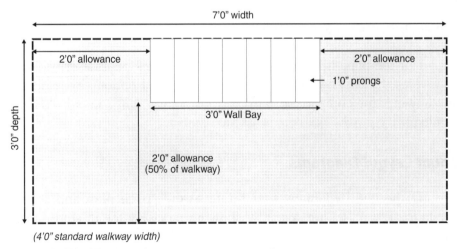

7'0" width

3'0" depth

2'0" allowance

2'0" allowance

1'0" prongs

3'0" Wall Bay

2'0" allowance
(50% of walkway)

(4'0" standard walkway width)

Shaded area indicates customer walkway

Total area = 7 x 3 = 21 sq ft

Total selling area (all stores) = 21 sq ft x 8 stores
= 168 sq ft

The space plan could then be prepared as set out below:

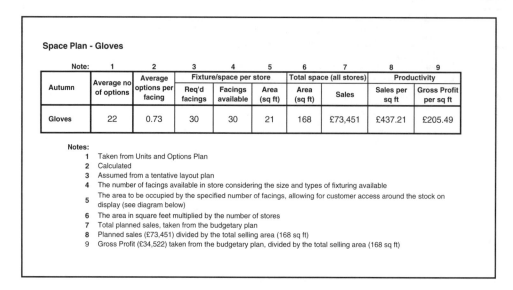

Space Plan - Gloves

Note:	1	2	3	4	5	6	7	8	9
Autumn	Average no of options	Average options per facing	Fixture/space per store			Total space (all stores)		Productivity	
			Req'd facings	Facings available	Area (sq ft)	Area (sq ft)	Sales	Sales per sq ft	Gross Profit per sq ft
Gloves	22	0.73	30	30	21	168	£73,451	£437.21	£205.49

Notes:
1. Taken from Units and Options Plan
2. Calculated
3. Assumed from a tentative layout plan
4. The number of facings available in store considering the size and types of fixturing available
5. The area to be occupied by the specified number of facings, allowing for customer access around the stock on display (see diagram below)
6. The area in square feet multiplied by the number of stores
7. Total planned sales, taken from the budgetary plan
8. Planned sales (£73,451) divided by the total selling area (168 sq ft)
9. Gross Profit (£34,522) taken from the budgetary plan, divided by the total selling area (168 sq ft)

The 3 documents: Budgetary Plan, Units & Options Plan and Space Plan combine to provide an overview of the range structure. We can look more deeply into the plan using other, more detailed documents to reveal greater range structure detail.

Units & Options by Price Point

This part of the plan stems from the units & options plan described above and provides the buyer with full details of units and options by retail price point showing, for comparison purposes last year's range detail. A sample schedule for the gloves example is set out opposite.

Product Layout Diagrams

These are the detailed plans that relate to the space plan and serve to illustrate the use of selling space by showing precisely the in-store location of the products. (See the layout plan for gloves illustrated earlier).

Having created our range structure plans using certain figures and assumptions, we can now review our model from a variety of different angles. We may want to challenge and change some of the assumptions to give a better end result. When we are satisfied that the plan makes good commercial sense, we can finalise it.

Units and Options Detail Plan

Department: Accessories   Season: Autumn

Section: Gloves

Price Points	LY Actual						Plan					
	No of styles	No of options	No of units	Mix	Value £	Value Mix	No of styles	No of options	No of units	Mix	Value £	Value Mix
2.99	4	14	6,100	66.3%	18,239	27.6%	3	11	6,800	62.1%	20,332	27.7%
3.50	2	4	456	5.0%	1,596	2.4%	1	3	800	7.3%	2,800	3.8%
3.99							1	1	288	2.6%	1,149	1.6%
4.99							1	1	240	2.2%	1,198	1.6%
9.99	1	1	900	9.8%	8,991	13.6%	1	1	1,020	9.3%	10,190	13.9%
19.99	2	4	1,500	16.3%	29,985	45.4%	2	3	1,500	13.7%	29,985	40.8%
25.99							1	2	300	2.7%	7,797	10.6%
29.99	1	1	240	2.6%	7,198	10.9%						
TOTAL	10	24	9,196	100.00%	66,009	100.00%	10	22	10,948	100.00%	73,451	100.00%

Average selling price: £7.18   Average selling price: £6.71

7. Range Profile

Having completed the plan, an important part of the process is to review the range profile critically from all angles to ensure the range structure has turned out the way we wanted.

Let's look at the aspects of range profile covered by the range structure plan:

- range width and stock depth – units & options plan
- price assortment – units & options per price point
- average selling price
- sales density.

Range Width and Stock Depth

Arithmetically, the concept of range width v. stock depth is a simple one. Application of the budgetary factors to the assumed average selling price of the range will generate a width and depth profile, but is it sensible? In terms of range width, there is one key question: how many options represent *real choice*? What is the point above which real choice becomes product duplication and causes confusion to the customer?

The stock depth issue is closely related to the budgeted rate of stockturn. How much stock depth is required in store will depend on two factors, display stock and back up. What is the minimum required display stock? How much back-up stock should be held in reserve? The issue of display stock depth begs the question: what is the minimum credible display stock level that should be presented to the customer in store? The issue of how much back-up stock it is necessary to hold will relate to the effectiveness of, and the method of, stock replenishment and must take account of supplier lead-time.

Price Assortment

The "good, better, best" principle is helpful here. Good, better, best relates to three main price bands, which will vary between different product areas but is equally applicable to all. The principle is the same. What percentage of the range falls into each price category?

Example			
	Good	**Better**	**Best**
Knitwear	£9.99 to £19.99	£24.99 to £39.99	Over £40
Units	5000	7650	1500
Mix (in units)	35%	54%	11%

Average Selling Price

The average selling price is an assumed figure, often based on the average selling price actually achieved in the same trading period the previous year. Last year's figure may be adjusted to reflect an overall upward or downward movement in price assortment.

Sales Density

In order to arrive at the planned sales density, assumptions and compromises will have been made and these should be reviewed. The assumptions on space required will be related to the use of certain types of fixturing. Can, or should, those fixtures be replaced with others that give better space utilisation?

The use of additional linear footage will improve the sales per square foot yield and thereby improve space productivity.

Compromises will be forced when the space required does not equal the space available, and a decision to use more or less space than the ideal needs to be made. Is the resultant sales density figure acceptable?

There are also some budgetary factors that form part of the range profile and these deserve closer examination, in particular, margin mix.

Margin Mix

Whilst it can easily be demonstrated that the range structure plan produces the required gross profit as shown in the buying budget, there is always a risk factor to be assessed. Range success is wholly dependent on sales success. Is the proposed stock investment high or low risk? How likely is it that the range will be successful? If we set aside the natural optimism felt by the buyer when constructing the range just for a moment, we need to consider whether the product is safe, core, basic product with a proven track record of sales success, or whether the product is high risk, perhaps highly fashionable or seasonal, and previously untried. The credibility of the margin mix will be under scrutiny.

8. Summary

In this chapter on range structure planning, we have considered the potential benefits of adopting a structured approach to range planning and the processes involved in producing such a plan and how to actually construct a plan. With the help of some sample formats, we have considered how we could publish the results of these deliberations. The next step in the buying cycle is to "put the meat on the bones" of the plan. We have a range structure and we have a buying budget. The buyer now has to select the merchandise that conforms to the requirements of the range structure and create a range plan. Where that product is going to come from is the subject of our next chapter on sources of supply!

Checklist

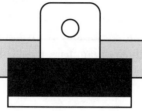

1. *The range structure plan combines budgetary and strategic criteria to create a shopping list for the buyer!*

2. *Range structure planning should take place before stock commitments are made.*

3. *The Range Structure Plan outlines the planned buy, whereas the Range Plan defines the actual buy.*

4. *Creating a range structure plan is rather like making a cake and, as with cake-making, what results is much more than just the sum of the separate ingredients.*

5. *Making decisions based on fact, and applying best skill and judgement is what management in general and buying in particular is all about!*

6. *Range width (as defined by the number of options), and range depth (as defined by the units per option), must conform to the total stock value requirement.*

7. *Having completed the plan, an important part of the process is to critically review the range profile from all angles to ensure the range structure has turned out the way we wanted.*

6

Sources of Supply

1. Introduction

Suppliers are a critical part of the retail industry, as few retailers manufacture their own products they are reliant upon suppliers for the products they sell. These products provide retailers with an opportunity to gain competitive advantage in their market and this makes retailers dependent upon their suppliers to ensure that the right products for their customers are available. In our enthusiasm to plan, budget, control and optimise sales and profits of the business it is sometimes easy to overlook this fact.

In this chapter we will look at:

- how a retailer decides how many suppliers to buy from
- the type of relationship that the company will develop with its suppliers
- how new suppliers can be found
- how this supply base is best managed by a structured approach to supplier evaluation and effective negotiation.

 Suppliers and retailers are essential to each other if either is to achieve their business objectives.

2. Supply Base Policy

A company's approach to its suppliers is determined by its supply base policy, which, as we saw in chapter two, forms part of the overall buying policy. This supply base policy will determine the number of suppliers, the type of relationship the company will have with its suppliers and the trading terms and conditions.

So what factors will influence the number of suppliers a retailer will buy from? The following are some of the possible considerations:

- the amount of variety needed within the product range
- the variety of product available from the suppliers
- the need to have a quick response to stock needs
- the size of the buying team – how many suppliers can be managed effectively?
- the facilities and staff required of the supplier to enable it to work effectively with the retailer
- the ease of setting up and maintaining supplier accounts
- the cost of dealing with each supplier
- the most cost effective quantity which needs to be ordered, sometimes referred to as the economic order quantity (EOQ).

Types of Suppliers – What's the difference?

Suppliers can vary from being wholesalers who buy from manufacturers and sell on their range, to being manufacturers who actually make the product; with some companies being both. The supply base policy may state the type of supplier you should buy from. Retailers without a warehousing function may prefer to work with wholesalers who can hold their stock, ensuring a regular supply of stock without the overhead of a warehouse. Larger retailers may find it more cost effective to work directly with the manufacturer but smaller companies may find the production volumes too large and it more cost effective to buy smaller quantities from a wholesaler, despite the additional margin the wholesaler will apply. In practice, many retailers work with both manufacturers and wholesalers in their search for the best product range.

Assignment 6:1 Consider your supply base and carry out a SWOT analysis

(SWOT analysis was described in Chapter 2 – Strengths, Weaknesses, Opportunities and Threats).

Examine each heading to assess the strengths and weaknesses of the supply base, and what are the opportunities and threats?

Case History

In 1990 Habitat developed a supply base policy of only buying from manufacturers in order to attain lower costs. The company had its own warehouses and therefore did not require wholesalers to hold the stock prior to delivery. They were also developing all their own product and did not require the design and development input which the wholesalers sometimes provided. The result was that the buying margin improved by 3%. However, the additional time involved in working directly with the manufacturer lead to considerable costs in time, travel and sampling expenses.

---

3. The Supplier Relationship – Adversaries or Partners?

Have you ever noticed how well people work when they are part of a team, sharing their knowledge and expertise? Some retailers ignore this and, because of their buying power, develop a domineering approach to their suppliers dictating terms and prices. This can be effective in getting the lowest prices, but will not make the supplier work harder to make the retailer successful. More enlightened retailers now see the potential in creating partnerships or teams with their suppliers. For example, BhS developed a supply base management team in order to work with their suppliers, to improve their business and their ability to supply BhS with the right products at the right time.

 Retailers and their suppliers both want the same thing: to sell more products to the end-consumer at a profit. Therefore, it makes sense to work together towards this common goal, maximising joint resources, market knowledge and experience.'

Partnership

Like any relationship, a partnership approach, whilst offering clear benefits, requires a greater level of commitment and increased openness in business dealings. The more time invested, the better the result. However time is always in short supply in retailing and many retailers who operate a partnership approach to their suppliers find that they can only work in this way with a smaller supply base. This, inevitably, places more business with the chosen suppliers making the relationship of more critical importance to both companies.

4. Sources of New Suppliers

As a buyer, you will always be on the look-out for new suppliers and there are several reasons why you may feel that new suppliers are needed.

- Existing companies may not be able to cope with the volume of your orders (although they may not find it easy to admit to this).
- A buyer may find that they do not have a suitable supplier in place for a particular product.
- They may want to double check that suppliers are offering competitive prices.
- A supplier may have gone out of business.
- A new company will need to find suitable suppliers to provide all their product range.

All these situations would lead a buyer to seek new suppliers. This search can be time consuming but fortunately several sources of new suppliers exist. The following are some of the most frequently used.

Trade Fairs

Every sector of the retail industry has a specialist trade fair, both in the UK and overseas, and many of the suppliers to that industry will exhibit. Trade fairs often provide a starting point in selecting new suppliers. Most trade fairs produce a catalogue and this can also provide a good reference guide to potential suppliers, for the rest of the year. Whilst at the trade fair, look at the products on display, the style, the prices and the quality to assess which companies you would like to talk to in more detail, but do not feel pressurised to make decisions on the spot. Other products not yet seen may eventually prove to be better suited to the range. Instead, make sure you collect all the relevant information and consider your decision away from the fair. Attending trade fairs is an integral expense of the buying department. UK Trade fairs are relatively inexpensive to attend, but overseas fairs can be much more costly. It is therefore important that a buyer makes the most of a fair.

 Use trade fairs as a way of assessing the potential of new suppliers, but take care not to get carried away with actual purchasing unless all the options have been considered.

Industry Journals

Journals and magazines produced for a market sector such as "Light" magazine and "Drapers Record" will contain advertisements and editorial features on many of the possible suppliers within the industry. Comparison over several editions will give a flavour of the main companies in the market. Many market sectors will also have a trade association which will give you leads to suppliers, e.g. the Lighting Association, which is useful to contact as they usually provide details of all their members and their key product areas. BSSA, with their knowledge of the retail industry, can also provide advice to their members on potential sources of supply. Some industries provide yearbooks with profiles. The Interior Designer's Handbook is one such yearbook which is an invaluable guide to retailers in the interior design market.

Direct Approaches

Sometimes you do not need to look for suppliers – sales representatives will contact *you*. Whilst there is rarely time to see all representatives, a file of interesting companies should be created to which the buyer can return when looking for new suppliers. A standard letter of reply, advising suppliers that you may not have an immediate need for their product, but that you may contact them at a later date, can save time and still retain their goodwill.

 Being approachable to new suppliers can also ensure that new developments are brought to the buyer's attention, as well as promotional opportunities such as special purchase products for a sale.

Competitors' Ranges – Learning From the Opposition

Regular reviews of competitors' ranges not only ensure that you are up to date on developments in your market, but also provide opportunities to find out more about their suppliers. As your knowledge of a market grows, the buyer will become aware of the source of many products in the marketplace and suppliers (sometimes unwittingly) help by adding their details onto the product or its packaging. The tracking down of the full supplier details may take a little detective work, but with a touch of "Sherlock Holmes" you may locate a potentially good supplier.

Buying Groups

Buying groups are independent companies who work with retailers as an extension of the buying department, undertaking much of the sourcing and development aspects of the buyer's role. Bloomingdales in the USA work with a large buying group, which has offices in all the key countries where product is selected. Bloomingdale buyers make their product selection from a range presented by the buying group.

Agents

Buying agents work as an interface between the buyer and the supplier. Sometimes they are employed by the supplier to act as a sales and marketing function and other times by the retailer, to source the best factories for the relevant product area, either by region, e.g. Italy or by product, e.g. stationery. Such agents take a considerable amount of legwork out of the search for a new supplier, although their involvement will typically add 5% to the cost prices.

Ad-Hoc Sources

Information about suppliers can sometimes come from the least expected sources.

- Colleagues may have contacts from previous experience.
- Existing suppliers will often discuss the industry and speak about new companies or their competitors.
- General magazines may include features on products or profiles of manufacturers.
- Television programmes may refer to sources of supply.

 Always be on the look out for new sources of supply. You never know when one will appear.

5. How to Manage Your Suppliers

We have looked at how you find new suppliers but how do you manage and develop your existing suppliers? Some larger companies now have separate departments called Supply Base Management to help the buyer monitor performance, be aware of the strengths and weaknesses of their suppliers and to ensure that the supply base works efficiently. This additional resource may also act as advisors to suppliers in order to develop and improve their business practices and sometimes their profitability. Obviously this resource costs money, but many retailers feel that it is a worthwhile investment to ensure the stability of their supply base. But what if your company does not have this resource – then it is down to you.

Supplier Evaluation Techniques

So how do you know if the supply base is working efficiently? The first step is for the buyer to review the suppliers' performance in a consistent manner on a regular basis. Many companies develop their own methods of evaluation, but the usual starting point is to determine the core skills which a supplier needs to possess and then to review how they perform against all of these key criteria. If some items are more important than others, then different weightings can be given. Adding it all up gives suppliers an overall score. The information which is used to complete the evaluation is both factual and anecdotal, although an emphasis upon factual evidence is important in order to prevent the evaluation becoming subjective.

Case History

Fred is a buyer of socks. He currently deals with three suppliers. Fred's business rates a supplier's delivery performance, quality and design above all other factors and these criteria are, therefore, given a higher weighting by senior management, as shown on the following table.

Over a period of time Fred collected evidence on the suppliers' performance against each of his criteria and gave each a score out of 10. This number was multiplied by the weighting. All the scores were then added together to give the final supplier score.

In this example suppliers 1002 and 1003 have identical scores unweighted, but applying the weighting makes 1003 the better supplier. Supplier 1001 performs the best overall but the weighting does reduce his score.

Supplier Evaluation Matrix

Weighting	1.2	1.2	1	0.7	1.2	0.8	0.9	
Criteria Supplier Ref No	Delivery Performance	Quality Performance	Innovation in New Product	Price	Design Capability	Commitment Level	Availablility of Key Personnel	Total
1001	7	8	6	9	7	8	9	54
	7 x 1.2 = 8.4	8 x 1.2 = 9.6	6 x 1.0 = 6.0	9 x 0.7 = 6.3	7 x 1.2 = 8.4	8 x 0.8 = 6.4	9 x 0.9 = 6.3	53.2
1002	4	5	9	8	9	8	7	50
	4 x 1.2 = 4.8	5 x 1.2 = 6.0	9 x 1.0 = 9.0	8 x 0.7 = 5.6	9 x 1.2 = 10.8	8 x 0.8 = 6.4	7 x 0.9 = 6.3	43.3
1003	9	9	5	6	4	8	9	50
	9 x 1.2 = 10.8	9 x 1.2 = 10.8	5 x 1.0 = 5.0	6 x 0.7 = 4.2	4 x 1.2 = 4.8	8 x 0.8 = 6.4	9 x 0.9 = 8.1	50.1

Maximum score = 70

Scores can be used to compare suppliers and to target specific low scoring areas for improvement. In extreme cases where the score is very low, the evaluation may result in the de-listing of a supplier. It is possible to evaluate each of the criteria separately using delivery or quality reports, but the evaluation matrix allows for an overall picture to be developed rather than reviewing core functions in isolation.

Regular reviews of supplier performance can target areas for improvement, and help the management of the supply base for both the retailer and the supplier.

6. Preparing for Supplier Meetings

To get the most out of any meeting you need to prepare thoroughly – as should your supplier. The time of both buyers and suppliers is valuable and in short supply, and it is important not to waste it by poor preparation. You are your company's representative with the supplier and any unprofessional behaviour reflects upon yourself and your company. How many times have we remembered some subject we intended to raise – but only after the meeting is over and the parties have split up.

Time invested in preparation for meetings will always pay off.

The following checklist can be used to ensure that you are properly prepared for your meetings.

Meetings Checklist

1. Ensure you have arranged a time and place for the meeting. This may involve having to book a meeting room.

2. Review the notes from the previous meeting.

3. Make sure you are familiar with the product they sell to you.

4. Review the sales performance of current products supplied by the company. Also review their delivery and quality record and the latest supplier evaluation.

5. Check with colleagues if there are any issues you need to be aware of prior to the meeting, e.g. disputed debit notes, late payments.

6. Set an agenda to ensure that you cover all the points you wish to discuss and distribute it prior to the meeting if you wish the supplier to prepare in advance.

7. After the meeting make notes and follow up on the key action or decision points.

---

7. Buying from Abroad – the Competitive Advantage?

Retailers are increasingly looking further afield in their search for products which will differentiate them from their competitors. Whilst potentially offering new products sometimes at lower cost prices, buying overseas may not always be the easy or suitable option.

The easiest way to buy from overseas is to use wholesale import companies who already have the experience and the infrastructure. Prices are usually around 20% higher than the delivered cost from a direct source, as wholesalers have to make their margin on the products, but a wider choice of products should be available and smaller orders are possible than buying direct. Delivery is usually the same as for a UK supplier, unless your company is ordering very large quantities which exceed the supplier's normal stockholding.

Direct Importing

Lower cost prices are always attractive to buyers and direct importing can help you to achieve this. The buyer works directly with the manufacturer and cost prices are lower than from the wholesaler. Unfortunately, it is not as simple as it first appears. The buyer's company usually takes responsibility for the freight of the products to the UK so specialists are needed within the company to ensure that products arrive safely. Payment may be requested by letters of credit (particularly from Far East suppliers) and again the retailer must be able to handle their administration.

To make buying direct from overseas cost effective, it is essential that the volume of your orders is large enough. Many Far East companies will only ship 20 foot containers – which can be a lot of product!

The further afield the supplier is, the more difficult it becomes to control the quality and delivery of the product. The culture of the country of origin may mean that, whilst it is not possible to generalise, business is conducted in a very different manner from the UK.

For example:

- Some buyers have experience of Japanese companies who have protracted negotiations for many hours
- Chinese companies have been known to promise what they could not deliver in order to secure an order and because they did not like to say "no"
- "Mañana" can be a way of life for some Spanish companies – always putting off until tomorrow what could be done today.

A solution to such potential problems for many companies is to use local agents to become their "eyes and ears" on the ground. Retailers who become committed to a particular overseas market may even establish their own buying office which provides a permanent point of contact, working solely on their behalf. The job of both agents and buying offices is to look for potential new suppliers, oversee product development, send samples and arrange the delivery and make relevant quality control checks. They can clearly take much of the risk and uncertainty out of buying overseas.

Agents and overseas buying offices can help to reduce the risk of direct importing.

Know the Real Cost

So is buying direct really cheaper? Certainly the initial comparison of a product's cost from a wholesaler versus buying direct from the manufacturer, will give an impression that direct importing will enable much higher margins to be achieved. But look a little further and the comparison may look less favourable.

Known On-Costs

Some additional costs will be known in advance. These include:

- freight costs
- duty as determined by Customs & Excise
- agents' fees.

The freight costs depend initially upon the terms of the cost price. An FOB cost price (free on board) means the goods are loaded onto the ship or plane. You will need to add the costs of the air or sea freight and transport from the UK airport or dock to your warehouse. Ex-works means that you pay the same costs as FOB, but you also pay to collect the goods from the factory. CIF (carriage, insurance and freight) means that the supplier arranges and pays for delivery to the UK dock or airport. This is less common and it is worth comparing their cost of freight with your own to make sure it is a competitive rate.

Sea freight is the slowest method of freight, taking 4-5 weeks from the Far East, but it is the cheaper option. Air freight is the other method, which is quicker but rather more expensive. Sometimes buyers use air freight where the cost to the business of lost sales is greater than the extra cost of the air freight.

Unknown On-Costs

Other costs cannot be foreseen in advance, but they can still seriously erode the margin. Despite the work of agents, products sometimes arrive in a condition which is unsaleable and you will have to arrange for the products to be reworked, returned or scrapped. Most Far Eastern containers are fumigated at the docks to eliminate uninvited "guests", however if this is not done a container, particularly of wood, may be infested with woodworm and will have to be sealed prior to treatment. In the meantime sales are being lost, new stock will not arrive in time to replace the initial delivery and you will have to try and negotiate compensation with a factory who are convinced that the goods left them in perfect condition.

Case History

A delivery of photo frames from India to a multiple retailer was found to have woodworm. The supplier denied responsibility saying the products were perfect. Unfortunately the crates in which the delivery was made had woodworm and during the long journey they had moved into the frames. Rentokill fumigated the container, but the goods had to be destroyed. After several weeks of negotiation the supplier agreed to replace the goods free of charge, but the retailer still had to pay for the freight on the faulty shipment. As a result of this the buyer increased the selling price and margin on such products to compensate for such unknown costs.

Communication costs are much higher when dealing overseas and frequently take up more management time than their UK counterparts. The Internet will reduce some of these costs eventually but its usage is not yet wide enough to have any great impact. Fax and telephone remain the main methods of communication However, it is rare for these communication costs to be attributed to the product.

 Always consider the direct and the indirect costs of direct import when comparing cost prices from overseas and UK sources.

8. Negotiation – Win-Lose or Win-Win?

Negotiation forms a large part of the communication with suppliers. Whilst negotiations will often concentrate on price or terms and conditions, the aim of negotiation is for you to get the best overall package for your business. To do this, you need to consider all the issues relating to the supplier's proposal. Negotiation will often take place with existing suppliers and can affect the long-term relationship with that supplier. A "win-lose" scenario may get you the deal you want but may also damage the relationship, and make future negotiations harder. The skilful negotiator manages to achieve a "win-win" scenario where both parties feel comfortable with the outcome; but the *very* skilled buyers manage to do this and get the terms they wanted.

Every negotiation goes through three stages: ***Preparation, Negotiation and Follow-up.***

Preparation

As any experienced buyer will tell you, the key to successful negotiating lies in the preparation.

Whilst burning the midnight oil may occasionally become necessary, careful management should ensure that most preparation can be made during normal working hours.

- You must know your facts – these include sales, delivery records, quality records, competitor retail prices, costs from other suppliers, previous price increases and the "bottom line" – the highest cost you can agree to. If you know more about the supplier's business than they know about yours, you will have an important advantage.
- Make sure you set the agenda and ensure the supplier sends through their proposals in advance.
- Consider what counter-arguments the supplier may make and how you will handle these.
- Try to determine which elements of the proposal are most important to the supplier.
- Work out where you can compromise and allow the supplier to win. If necessary add some additional requests which you will be prepared to concede.

- Make sure you have sufficient time and a suitable location.
- In difficult negotiations arrange the meeting on your premises.
- Do not have lunch with a supplier **prior** to a key negotiation as it can make you feel compromised.
- Never be afraid to ask for additional management support if the negotiation warrants it.

The Negotiation

- Stay in control. Work to your agenda.
- The negotiation is not personal. Do not get angry or flustered.
- Listen to their point of view. Even if you do not concede on this issue it will make your decision appear considered.
- Do not concede any points unless you have been given something of equivalent value in return.
- Keep an open mind.
- Summarise all points agreed at the end of the negotiation.
- Take your time, do not feel you have to resolve everything immediately, a follow-up meeting can always be called.

The Follow-up

- Confirm all points agreed in writing. Keep notes for future negotiations.
- Do not go back on an agreement and do not allow a supplier to ignore the agreement.
- Review your performance. Did it go as planned? How could it have been better?

 Negotiation is an important buying skill and every buyer should endeavour to improve their skills through training.

9. Terms of Supply/Contract

Your company will probably have their own terms and conditions of purchase and all your suppliers will have theirs. So how do these combine? Large companies can dictate their terms, but smaller companies will need to negotiate with suppliers.

Most retailers try to ease cash flow by paying for products as long as possible after delivery. Payment terms can vary from 7 to 120 days, and a company policy usually exists to guide buyers. Suppliers want to be paid as quickly as possible. One option which offers a compromise is to offer a discounted payment for the reduction of the payment period, along the following lines:

>   normal payment terms – nett 30 days
>   negotiated terms 5% settlement discount for 10 days payment

However, suppliers who are aware of the settlement discount will often add it onto their cost price and many retailers now prefer to opt for a net payment, with an industry acceptable time period of 30 days.

Battle of the Forms

Every buyer needs to be aware that the terms and conditions of supply which apply in law are those on the last document which carries the terms and conditions. These may be yours or your supplier's. This is often referred to as the "Battle of the Forms" – for more details refer to the BSSA book, *Law for Retailers*. The buyer's terms will normally be printed onto their order, which would seem to cover the problem, but what if the supplier's terms are printed onto the order acknowledgement making theirs the terms which apply? Clearly this could be a problem and to overcome this, buyers need to ensure that they have a clear agreement in writing to their terms and conditions.

Assignment 6:2 Supplier issues

Now try our multi-choice questionnaire, overleaf, which deals with issues related to Chapter 6.

Please put each statement in priority order, i.e. 1 = statement you feel to be most important/correct; 4 = statement you feel to be least important/ correct

The correct marking scale is shown in Appendix 2.

---

1. A buyer's relationship with a supplier should be:

	1	2	3	4
a) Adversarial	☐	☐	☐	☐
b) Relaxed and friendly	☐	☐	☐	☐
c) A professional partnership	☐	☐	☐	☐
d) As determined by the supply base policy	☐	☐	☐	☐

2. How is the supply base best managed?

	1	2	3	4
a) By regular meetings with suppliers	☐	☐	☐	☐
b) By a formal process of supplier evaluation	☐	☐	☐	☐
c) By the supply base management team	☐	☐	☐	☐
d) By ad-hoc reviews	☐	☐	☐	☐

3. A new supplier may be found by:

	1	2	3	4
a) Looking in trade journals	☐	☐	☐	☐
b) Word of mouth	☐	☐	☐	☐
c) Advertising	☐	☐	☐	☐
d) Trade fairs	☐	☐	☐	☐

4. Which of the following points are important to include in a supplier evaluation?

	1	2	3	4
a) The supplier's delivery record	☐	☐	☐	☐
b) How much you like the personnel	☐	☐	☐	☐
c) The quality of the product	☐	☐	☐	☐
d) How often they take you to lunch	☐	☐	☐	☐

5. A retailer may decide to buy direct from an overseas source because:

	1	2	3	4
a) The retailer has more control over the product development	☐	☐	☐	☐
b) The buyers like to travel	☐	☐	☐	☐
c) The products are cheaper	☐	☐	☐	☐
d) They have their own import department	☐	☐	☐	☐

6. A buyer can be successful in negotiation by:

	1	2	3	4
a) Only conceding a point when offered something in return	☐	☐	☐	☐
b) Preparing thoroughly	☐	☐	☐	☐
c) Allowing the supplier to control the agenda	☐	☐	☐	☐
d) Working towards a win-win scenario	☐	☐	☐	☐

See Appendix 1 for marking scale

11. Summary

In this chapter we have looked at:

- the ways in which buying policy will determine the supply base
- the types of suppliers which exist
- the type of relationship which a retailer may have with their suppliers
- sources of new suppliers and the reasons why new suppliers may be required
- how to evaluate the supply base to ensure that the right suppliers are working efficiently to help the retailer gain competitive advantage.

In the next chapter we will look at the most crucial part of the buyer's responsibility, the product and how to plan the range and undertake the product development.

Checklist

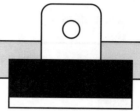

1. Suppliers and retailers are essential to each other if either is to achieve their business objectives.

2. Retailers and their suppliers both want the same thing, to sell more products to the end-consumer at a profit. It, therefore, makes sense to work together towards this common goal, maximising joint resources, market knowledge and experience.

3. Use trade fairs as a way of assessing the potential of new suppliers, but take care not to get carried away with the actual purchasing unless all the options have been considered.

4. Being approachable to new suppliers can also ensure that new developments are brought to the buyer's attention, as well as promotional opportunities such as special purchase products for a sale.

5. Always be on the look out for new sources of supply. You never know when one will appear.

6. Regular reviews of supplier performance can target areas for improvement, and help the management of the supply base for both the retailer and the supplier.

7. Time invested in preparation for meetings will always pay off.

8. To make buying direct from overseas cost effective, it is essential that the volume of your orders is large enough. Many Far East companies will only ship 20 foot containers – which can be a lot of product!

9. Agents and overseas buying offices can help to reduce the risk of direct importing.

10. Always consider the direct and the indirect costs of direct import when comparing cost prices from overseas and UK sources.

11. As any experienced buyer will tell you, the key to successful negotiating lies in the preparation.

12. Whilst burning the midnight oil may occasionally become necessary, careful management should ensure that most preparation can be made during normal working hours.

13. Negotiation is an important buying skill and all buyers should endeavour to improve their skills through training.

7

Range Planning and Product Development

1. Introduction

The product range is the central focus of any buyer's activities and the appeal of the range to the customer will make the difference between success and failure. So, as we saw in chapter five, it is critical that the right products are selected or developed and that it is carried out in a controlled way. Range planning provides the buyer with a framework within which they can manage the development of the product range and better guarantee its success. The framework is illustrated below:

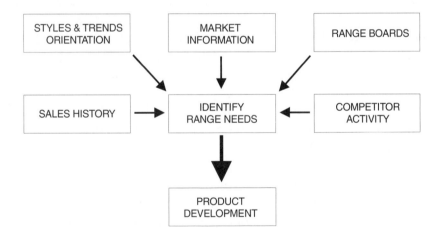

In this chapter we will look at:

- the development of the range plan and how to identify range needs
- the process by which products are selected or specifically developed to meet these identified range needs
- how buyers can ensure that the product ordered is the product which is delivered by the development of product specifications.

A planned product range has a much greater chance of success than an unplanned one.

2. Identification of Range Needs

So how do you decide which products will be included in the product range? In most cases, a range will already exist, but to improve sales or refresh the offer, it will need to be revised. The first task with an existing range would be to undertake a detailed sales analysis on the current products. This will identify those products which are successful and those which are not.

Assignment 7:1 The Stars and the Dogs

Some retailers call their successful products "stars" and the failures "dogs". Consider a current range within your business; which are the stars and which are the dogs?

What benchmark did you use to judge them against, e.g. below/above average sales, comparison to the sales plan?

The exact definition of success or failure will vary depending upon the size of company and the type of product. Clearly a large chain of stores will expect higher sales from their products than an independent retailer with only one outlet.

This sales analysis should also refer back to the original sales plan and budget. Did the current product selection allow you to achieve these targets? If not, which lines failed to perform? Chapter 9 will examine the review of sales performance in more detail and the criteria which can be used to evaluate the reasons for poor performance.

The sales analysis should create an understanding of which products are successful and why. Is it their colour, size, price point, material, style or a combination of several of these?

Sales analysis therefore, allows future development to build upon previous knowledge and ensures that product mistakes whilst never eliminated (as every range has its successes and failures) are at least minimised.

 Build on product successes and learn from product failures.

In an existing range, poor performing products should be discontinued from the range creating spaces for new product introductions, otherwise the size of the range will increase each season and the stores will be filled with products which do not sell. The number of products which will be replaced each season is defined by the range refreshment policy. This policy will be individual to your company or department and is usually influenced by the type of products sold. For example, fashion retailers may change 80% of their range each season, whereas a homewares retailer may only change 10%. The reason for this difference is primarily that fashion products will date more quickly and they are also linked to the Season of the year. No UK buyer would normally try to sell bikinis in volume at Christmas or wool coats in June.

If the product range is completely new, no sales figures will be available, which can make life a bit more difficult. However, a buyer may be able to estimate sales based on the sales of other products within the business. Alternatively, suppliers should be able to provide information on typical sales trends for particular products.

Case History

A retail shop within a new London Attraction wanted to include T-shirts in their range. These T-shirts were to carry the logo of the Attraction and be sold in 5 colours, across 4 sizes. The buyer chose black, white, grey, blue and red. However, after consulting with the supplier on sales from other similar retail outlets, red was dropped as a potentially poor seller, but orders of black and white were increased in order to maximise the potential sales.

---

3. Range Boards

The increasing sophistication of technological methods of sales analysis allows buyers to go into great depth with their analysis, but sometimes too much detail can divert the focus away from the product itself.

Customers buy products from ranges sold in store and they assess the range primarily on its physical appeal, linked with its value for money. It is therefore vital that buyers always consider what the range looks like and the physical attributes of all products, both successes and failures. However, to have all the current products available in an area close to the buyer's desk is often impractical, so range boards comprising photographs of every product, arranged by style and/or price point, are frequently used to provide an overview of the product range.

Range boards help new buyers to learn a product range quickly and can also be useful if new products have to be presented to senior managers, as they can show that the new products have been developed within the context of an overall range.

4. Competitors

A key element of developing a product range is to ensure that it will appeal to the retailer's target customer, and will be sufficiently differentiated from the competition to ensure that customers are attracted to your stores. The only way to ensure this, is to have a thorough knowledge of what your competitors currently sell and this involves undertaking regular reviews of those who have been identified as key competitors. The table opposite provides a basic framework for competitor reviews, which can be adapted to suit specific needs of any company.

Competitors may also inspire product development within the buyer's own range, by selling new products which are omitted from the current range, or by indicating – through the volume of stock – that a product area is very successful. One word of caution on this is to try and ensure that the range is not a "dog" about to be reduced for clearance! Casual conversation with staff may sometimes reveal the truth of this or, alternatively, suppliers may be able to advise on the range's success or failure.

5. Market Information

Part of reviewing the competition also includes studying the current trends in the market. This will help a buyer to decide which product area to expand or contract to ensure that the range has maximum appeal to the customer. For example, if you were a buyer of domestic lighting and you know that the housing market was in decline, you may decide to move the emphasis of the range away from fixed lighting and into portable lighting. Likewise, if you knew that bright colours were very fashionable you may decide to introduce more new lines, with bright colours into the business.

 Use market information to ensure that the range meets customer needs and tastes.

COMPETITOR NAME	*Beds R Us*		DATE OF REVIEW	*Sep-99*
PRODUCT AREA	*100% cotton sheets*			

NUMBER OF PRODUCT LINES	LOWEST PRICE POINT	HIGHEST PRICE POINT
28	£6.99	£19.99

PRICES OF COMPARABLE PRODUCTS

Single cotton sheet	£6.99	Single Egyptian cotton sheet	£9.99
Double cotton sheet	£8.99	Double Egyptian cotton sheet	£14.99
King cotton sheet	£9.99	King Egyptian cotton sheet	£19.99

KEY STRENGTHS	KEY WEAKNESSES
Ranges displayed by style and colour	Poor packaging
Clear point of sale signage with features and benefits of ranges	

PROMOTIONAL ACTIVITY	KEY CHANGES FROM PREVIOUS REVIEW (date)
Value packs 2 x single sheets and 4 x pillowcase at £14.99	Introduction of Egyptian range

So, market trends may be related to the economy or to fashion. The economy is easy to monitor through the press and your industry. Fashion trends can be identified by looking at designer stores, magazines or at trade fairs. Some companies use trend consultants to help them to identify the latest styles and colours but, as this can prove very expensive, their use is usually limited to the major retailers.

6. Orientation for Product Sourcing and Development

Once you've analysed the performance of a product range, and identified the number of options which need to be discontinued and know the number of options which need to be introduced, the next stage is to decide the type and style of new products. This may be done using the skills of the individual buyer, but some companies now use the process of product orientation.

A product orientation provides a visual direction to the buyer of the style and colours of the products to be developed. Product orientations are particularly valuable to larger companies where different product ranges are bought by different buyers. The orientation will illustrate, often on storyboards, the key styles, themes and colour palette for the season. This ensures that all the buyers are working to the same criteria and that when the products eventually arrive in store, they will co-ordinate and appear as one cohesive offer to the customer.

However, it is not only the larger companies who can benefit from product orientation, smaller companies can also benefit by taking the time to consider the styles of their products and the colour palettes.

 Even small ranges will benefit from some co-ordination which will help to make the range individual to your company and appear unified to the customer.

7. Core and Fashion Ranges

The orientation process may divide the products into core and fashion ranges. The core range is essentially the "bread and butter" element, with products which sell consistently over a long period and are little affected by fashion trends. The fashion range, as its name implies, is likely to change more frequently and is clearly influenced by style and colour trends.

The Range Pyramid

A progression from dividing the range into core and fashion is to divide it into sections with a range pyramid, as follows:

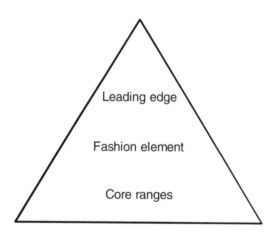

The size of each section is determined by the type of business and the product type. The lowest section is the core range, the basics – it is the white T-shirt to the fashion retailer, or the pack of five ladies briefs to Marks & Spencer. Nearly every range has a core element, but the size of this will vary.

The next section is the fashion element, which will change more frequently, and the final section is the leading edge, the "pzazz" in the buyer's range. Leading-edge product is included to attract the customers' interest and sometimes that of the press. It can change frequently to maintain customer interest and, because of its higher risk, it may attract a higher margin than may be applied to core or fashion products. But, be careful, leading-edge products are only the "icing on the cake". It is easy to get distracted by more exciting products, but you need to address the rest of the range first.

 A retailer's money is made on the "cake" and not on the "icing".

8. Product Development Versus Product Sourcing

The difference between product development and sourcing is often not apparent, but essentially product development involves the design and development of original products, whereas product sourcing involves selecting products which are already developed by the suppliers.

The reasons why a company may select one approach or another may vary, and some companies may combine the two. Advantages and disadvantages of product development sourcing are shown on the table below:

	ADVANTAGES	DISADVANTAGES
Product development	Exclusive Range	Cost of development resource
	Differentiate from opposition	Time of development, 3 to 12 months
	Develop brand identity	Minimum orders may be higher
	Less opportunities for price comparison	Potential tooling/ origination charges
Product selection	Speed	No differentiation from opposition
	No origination costs	Litle or no exclusivity
	No resource needed to finalise product	Easy to compare prices
	Product available immediately	Induces little loyalty in customers

Case History

In 1994 an independent London retailer increased their sales of toiletries by developing their own range. The product was the same as before but a different colour bottle and new label made it unique to that retailer, proving that product development does not have to involve starting from nothing and that even the smallest companies can develop their own ranges.

9. Practicalities of Product Development

Product development clearly has benefits for retailers provided that they can justify the time and cost of the development process. But where does a buyer start? The first stage is to know what you are trying to develop.

Briefing Designers

The new products may require a designer to develop ideas or to take them forward into drawings. These may be sketches or technical drawings – depending upon the requirements of the manufacturer.

When briefing a designer, the following points need to be considered in the brief, if the designer is to produce a meaningful response.

- State how many individual products you need.
- What retail and/or cost prices are you targeting?
- What materials had you envisaged?
- What size should the products be?
- Where will the products fit into the existing range?
- Are there specific functions you want the product to perform? (e.g. dishwasher safe)
- What sort of drawings do you require, sketches or technical drawings?
- Does the product have to co-ordinate with anything else? (e.g. the shoes with the handbag)
- Are there any display or packaging criteria the designer needs to know?
- Are there any manufacturing restrictions on the design? (e.g. minimum quantities)

 The more you can tell the designer the more suited the design will be for your product range.

Briefing Suppliers

Increasingly, in response to retailers' demands, suppliers employ their own designers and the briefing of the designer and the supplier may happen at the same time. However, if the two are separate, the supplier will need to be briefed. This briefing may involve two stages – feasibility and detailed discussion.

Feasibility may include the cost of the development in terms of production time and tooling costs; the minimum quantity which needs to be produced and the timescale for development. The product will obviously not be feasible if development takes 6 months and you need the product on sale in 6 weeks!

The second stage will involve discussing the designs with the supplier. It is often easier to involve the designers in this process as they will know why elements were designed in a particular way. Also if anything needs to be changed to make the design more practical or economical to manufacture, the designer can help to adapt the design without losing its core elements.

Supplier Capabilities

Some suppliers can develop product for a retailer and some cannot, due to their staff resources and manufacturing facilities. The buyer needs to assess which ones are suitable. Knowledge of the supply base is critical in this assessment as considerable time can be wasted if the selected supplier finally proves to be unsuitable. Some suppliers can worsen the situation by agreeing to produce products despite the fact that it is not within their capabilities. A fear of losing business by saying " no" to a buyer, particularly a buyer from a large company, can cause the supplier to act in this way. Knowledge of the supplier should enable a buyer to see through such over-optimism.

Time Available

The timescale for the introduction of the product may dictate whether product development is possible, and which supplier is the most suitable. A supplier in China may be able to produce the product for less, but if it is 6 months after you want it delivered, an alternative European source at a slightly higher cost may prove the better option.

Ideally, the product development process should be planned sufficiently in advance to allow the buyer complete freedom in the choice of manufacturer. Some companies work up to two years ahead in order to ensure that the product development has sufficient time and many major retailers work 12 months in advance.

Is it Cost Effective?

Sometimes the development costs of the new product are disproportionate to the anticipated product sales. A new product may cost £5,000 to develop. If its sales plan was £50,000 this may be felt to be acceptable, but if the sales plan is £8,000 then obviously it would not be sensible to continue. It is therefore vital that a buyer knows the sales plan for a product in order to assess the cost-effectiveness of developing a new product.

A similar situation can occur with minimum order requirements. It is no good developing a product with a minimum order of 10,000 units if all you need to order is 1,000 units!

In such circumstances, if the product is vital to your range, it may need to be sourced rather than developed, although changes to the packaging and labelling can still help to make it appear exclusive to your company.

Cost Recovery

Where a product does incur origination charges in tooling, new moulds, or packaging, these costs need to be covered by sales of the product. Some companies have a separate budget for product origination charges which makes life easier. But what if this doesn't exist? Then the origination charge has to be built in to the product cost. Typically the cost is spread across, or "amortised" over an agreed number of units, e.g.

Origination charge	£1,000.00
Product costs price	£10.00
Quantity bought	10,000
Amortised cost	$\dfrac{£1,000.00 + £10.00}{10,000} = £10.10$

The additional cost of 10p is calculated by dividing the origination charge by the quantity bought. This figure is then added to the original cost price. In this instance the origination charge can be recovered without adversely affecting the cost of the product.

Assignment 7:2 Amortisation

If 5,000 units of a product are bought for £13.43 each with a tooling charge of £278 what is the new amortised cost of:

a)   5,000 units?

b)   10,000 units?

c   2,000 units?

(Answer at end of chapter)

 Always ensure that once the origination charges have been paid, the cost price reverts to the lower figure, otherwise the supplier will gain an extra margin at the buyer's expense.

Sampling

Any product which is developed will need to be sampled at least once before it is purchased. It is vital that the buyer checks that the product is as they want it. Many products can look great on paper but disastrous when finally produced. It is not unusual for the first sample to be rejected, if not the second or third. The buyer must ensure the supplier is aware of this from the outset to avoid any confusion at a later date.

Trialling

There are many potential pitfalls with introducing new products. There are costs and risks involved in the process. For example – what happens if the product dose not sell? Some retailers whose level of investment in a new product is high or who are reliant on only a few products will often trial a new product prior to going into full production.

So what are the advantages or disadvantages of trialling?

TRIALLING

Advantages

Lower risk.

Learn about the product performance before committing to higher quantities.

Don't have to discontinue existing product before buying in the replacement.

The value of the product line can be more accurately assessed.

Disadvantages

Potentially higher unit costs for producing a smaller quantity.

Trial may not give a proper indication of the sales pattern.

Competitors may see and copy new developments.

Customers perceive it as a lack of conviction by the retailer in the product – so don't buy.

Stores have to be able to cope with trialling.

The results of the trial have to be interpreted correctly if they are to be of use in the making of future product decisions.

Trialling therefore, can minimise risk and lead to better product decisions, but the process has to be properly managed, otherwise the potential benefits involved do not outweigh the cost.

Case History

A large retailer wanted to assess the potential of including a small electrical range within their kitchen department. A range was sold in 3 stores but because the products lacked the correct labels the sales data was not captured accurately and the trial proved inconclusive.

Packaging

Packaging and labelling are an integral part of the product, often forgotten until the last minute. The correct packaging can enhance the product, convey vital information to the customer and promote the brand as well as protecting the product in transit and in store. The type and design of the packaging needs to be considered alongside the development of the product and its costs considered in the same way as the product development costs. However, as a result of recent legislation, buyers also need to confirm to suppliers how the packaging will be disposed of and then re-cycled. The UK will soon have to conform to the laws on packaging and recycling which are evident in some other European countries.

Chapter 11, Presenting the Product, includes a more in-depth consideration of the purpose of packaging and the logistics of its development.

Product Specifications

It is a vital element of the buyer's role that the product which has been developed or sourced is identical to the product which is consistently delivered. But what happens if this is not the case? How do you prove that the supplier has made an error, particularly if they deny making any changes?

One method is to produce product specifications for all the products purchased. These will vary between companies and product areas, but they should all include details of the physical properties of the product, its size and material content. Textile products may also include weight and weave construction; clothing products would include detailed size specifications and some products, such as lighting or toys, would also include their certificate of conformity to the relevant legislation to prove that they are safe for sale in the UK.

An example of a product specification for a giftware retailer is detailed below:

GIFT RETAILER PRODUCT SPECIFICATION

SUPPLIER DETAILS

SUPPLIER	A Supplier Limited		
ADDRESS:	Any Street	CONTACT NAME:	Mr Smith
	Anywhere	TITLE:	Sales Manager
	Any Town		
		TEL:	01234 567890
POSTCODE:	AB5 6DE	FAX:	01234 567098
		EMAIL:	a.supplier.com

PAYMENT TERMS		BUYING TERMS	
CURRENCY:	US Dollars	TERM:	FOB
PAYMENT TERM:	Nett 30 days		
PAYMENT METHOD:	Telegraphic transfer	PLACE:	HONG KONG

LEAD TIME	
SUPPLIER:	60 DAYS
FREIGHT:	28 DAYS
TOTAL:	88 DAYS

PRODUCT SPECIFICATION

SUPP REF	CODE	PRODUCT NAME	COLOUR/ MATERIAL
A3140	370506	CHLOE TEAPOT	CREAM/CERAMIC

COSTINGS						
COST:	£4.30	RETAIL:	£11.99	RETAIL EX VAT: £10.20	MARGIN EX VAT:	57.8%

PRODUCT SPECIFICATION
1 LITRE CERAMIC TEAPOT IN CREAM SATIN GLAZE
DESIGN: CHLOE

CARE INSTRUCTIONS
DISHWASHER SAFE
MICROWAVE SAFE

ON-COSTS					
			FREIGHT:	£0.70	
AGENT:	£0.25	ORIG/N £ -	OTHER:	£ -	
ROYALTY:	£ -	PACKAGING £ -	TOTAL:	£0.95	

COUNTRY OF ORIGIN	CHINA

EXCLUSIVE	YES

PACKAGING DETAILS		
INNER PACK:	POLYBAG AND CARD BOX	ISSUE UNIT: 4.00
OUTER PACK:	CARD TRANSIT BOX	

LABELLING DETAILS			
PRODUCT	SWING TICKET	INNER PACK:	INNER LABEL
		OUTER PACK	OUTER LABEL

DISPOSABLE PACKAGING DETAILS					
MATERIAL TYPE	-	PAPER/FIBREBOARD	WEIGHT	0.25	IN WHOLE KILOGRAMS
MATERIAL TYPE	-	GLASS	WEIGHT		IN WHOLE KILOGRAMS
MATERIAL TYPE	-	ALUMINIUM	WEIGHT		IN WHOLE KILOGRAMS
MATERIAL TYPE	-	STEEL	WEIGHT		IN WHOLE KILOGRAMS
MATERIAL TYPE	-	PLASTIC	WEIGHT	0.01	IN WHOLE KILOGRAMS
MATERIAL TYPE	-	WOOD	WEIGHT		IN WHOLE KILOGRAMS
MATERIAL TYPE	-	OTHER MATERIALS	WEIGHT		IN WHOLE KILOGRAMS

Always ensure that the suppliers sign off the specification to prove that they agree with all the details. They may otherwise question the accuracy of the specification if a dispute arises.

Some companies retain a "Gold Seal" sample of the product prior to the first delivery. The sample is part of the delivery and is used as a benchmark to ensure that future deliveries conform to the specification of the first delivery. This can work better than written specifications but, as these samples take up considerable space, even companies who opt for this method sometimes find it easier to keep written specifications in the office.

10. Summary

In this chapter we have looked at the core element of the buyer's role – the development of the product range (either through product development or through sourcing.) The "correct" route for the company will depend upon the individual retailer, the timescale, costs and resources. However the range is created, it is vital that it is undertaken with a managed approach to ensure that it matches the criteria (either financial or aesthetic) laid down in the buying policy. The product range can work to define the retailer's image, and this image and the development of brands, is the subject of the next chapter.

ANSWER TO ASSIGNMENT 2:

a)	£13.49
b)	£13.46
c)	£13.57

Checklist

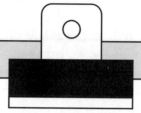

1. A planned product range has a much greater chance of success than an unplanned one.

2. Build on product successes and learn from product failures.

3. Range boards help new buyers to learn a product range quickly and can also be useful if new products have to be presented to senior managers, as they can show that the new products have been developed within the context of an overall range.

4. Use market information to ensure that the range meets customer needs and tastes.

5. Even small ranges will benefit from some co-ordination which will help to make the range individual to your company and appear unified to the customer.

6. A retailer's money is made on the "cake" and not on the "icing".

7. The more you can tell the designer the more suited the design will be for your product range.

8. Always ensure that once the origination charges have been paid the cost price reverts to the lower figure, otherwise the supplier will gain an extra margin at the buyer's expense.

9. Always ensure that the suppliers sign off the specification to prove that they agree with all the details. They may otherwise question the accuracy of the specification if a dispute arises.

8

Brand Development

1. Introduction

Brands have been around for many years in our shops – think of brands such as Heinz, Levi Jeans and Pears Soap. Many of these manufacturers' brands still exist, but today it is not only manufacturers who develop brands. Retailers are now taking a lead and developing brands of their own.

In this chapter we will look at:

- what is meant by a brand
- how it can be used to benefit a retail business
- how it can be used by buyers on their product and its packaging
- how it can be used to promote the product range.

2. What Is a Brand?

The term "brand" is often used in retailing, but what do we mean by a brand? Traditionally it was a name used to identify a particular product, such as Oxo or Hoover, but now a brand is generally viewed as more than this. It can be an identity which encompasses not only the product but all aspects of the company, the store interiors, the sales staff, the logo and stationery and even the management style.

The brand name may be the same as the company name, such as "Tesco", or it may be a separate name, such as "St. Michael" at Marks & Spencer. Either way, it serves the same purpose and aims to identify the product to the customer and to differentiate the product and the company from its competitors.

The brand has its own identity, an identity which is created by its association with specific values. These values, when communicated to the customer can create a specific view of the product or the retailer in the eyes of the customer. (For example, the development of the "George" range of clothing at Asda has enabled a food retailer to become a dominant player in the childrenswear market).

 A brand should have a unique identity which is easily recognised by the customer.

The table below illustrates some well-known retail brands and the values which can be associated with them.

Retailer	Brand Name	Values
Marks & Spencer	St. Michael	Quality, classic styling, middle class, reliable, trustworthy.
Ikea	Ikea	Stylish design, low price, young, trendy, Swedish.
Sainsbury	Sainsbury	Fresh, value for money, choice, reliable, traditional.

Some brand values are perceived as more important than others. The most important brand values are called core brand values and the less important are called secondary brand values. For example, The core brand values for Ikea would be "stylish design, low price and Swedish". "Young and trendy" would be secondary brand values. It is essential for the management and development of the brand that the core values are conveyed by all the activities of the business. Secondary brand values can be used more discriminatingly.

Assignment 8:1 Brand names

Now complete the same exercise for your own business. If there is not a separate brand name, consider the company name.

Try to determine the core and secondary values for your business. Make sure that the values reflect the current situation rather than what you would like them to be.

---

3. Primary and Secondary Brands

Most retailers only have one brand, but some companies may need additional or secondary brands. The values of a brand have to appeal to the target customer, and some businesses, such as department stores, may have a diverse customer base who cannot all be encompassed by a single brand. House of Fraser uses the Fraser brand as a primary brand, but then has developed secondary brands for particular target markets for example, "Linea" for young male and female fashions and "Platinum" for older female fashion customers.

4. Benefits of Brands

Now we have defined a brand, we can consider how it can benefit a retailer.

Differentiation

A key benefit of a brand is that it has its own identity and can be recognised by the customer as unique. The amount of competition on the high street is increasing rapidly and customers have far more choice than ever before. If they are able to identify your products and perceive them as different from the competition, then they will be more likely to spend their money with you.

 Brands can help to generate sales revenue when they are clearly defined and targeted at specific customers.

Costs and Pricing

This sense of uniqueness also prevents direct price comparisons with other retailers. Whilst this does not mean that a company should stop offering value for money, it does mean that the customer will not be as aware of the price for the product, and some opportunities for margin improvement will exist.

 The development of a brand can allow for higher margins to be achieved.

The attachment of brand values onto a product can increase the retail price which the customer is willing to pay. For example, a "Jaeger" jacket could retail for a higher price than a "Debenhams" own-label jacket, even if they were identical because of the values associated with the "Jaeger" brand.

The development of own-brands by supermarkets was originally intended to offer lower prices than the premium manufactured brands, such as Heinz or Kelloggs. The manufacturer did not have to carry the costs of marketing the supermarket brand and often some supermarkets' branded products are lower priced than the manufacturers' brands. However, as the supermarket brands develop a reputation of their own, such price differentiation is becoming less obvious.

Customer Loyalty

What brand of baked beans do you buy? Are you consistent in your choice? Many customers are very loyal and will buy the same brand for years. This loyalty is earned by the brand, by it consistently offering a certain set of values which appeal to the customer. It takes a significant change in the product or the customer for this loyalty to be broken. "Perrier" lost significant market share in the UK when its sparkling water was found to be contaminated by carcinogenic benzine – all stock was removed from sale until "safe" products could be reintroduced. Without this health scare, it would probably still be the premium brand.

 Brands can generate customer loyalty but loyalty is built on trust. If the trust is broken then so is the customer loyalty.

Customer loyalty is keenly sought by retailers as it converts into consistent sales year after year. This consistency has benefits to the buyer who can negotiate with suppliers from a position of strength to gain better prices, terms, quality and flexibility.

Marketing Opportunities

The existence of a brand provides opportunities for a marketing approach which does not have to rely on specific products. This approach can provide benefits to the whole business and has potentially broader appeal than specific product-focused marketing. Established brands are immediately recognisable to the consumer, conjuring up a host of associated values. For example, the Golden "M" of McDonalds immediately brings to mind the brand values of consistency, efficiency and convenience.

The brand has intrinsic values which differentiate it from other brands. However, none of these values will be effective if they are not:

- Supported by the customer's experience
- Valued by the customer.

If a retail brand conveys values of premium product and high quality, and the customer experiences poorly made product, sold in a chaotic store environment by slovenly sales staff, then the brand values will be at such variance to reality as to make them worthless.

If the customer wants a low cost, self-service retailer, they will not appreciate the brand values of an expensive, high service retailer and the brand values will be effectively wasted on this customer.

 Brand values have to be valued by the customer or they will fail to generate the anticipated product sales.

Assignment 8:2 Brand values

In the first column state your current brand values and in the second state what your customers want from your brand. Are there any discrepancies? You could change your brand values or change your customer, but as it is easier to keep a customer than gain a new one, it is better for you to change.

Current Brand Values	Customers' Expectations of Brand

5. Communication of the Brand

Communication Through Product

The most obvious way to identify a brand on a product is to place the brand name or logo physically on the product! Whilst this can work well for clothing it may not be desirable to have a blatant brand name on an item of soft-furnishing.

However, the brand can still be conveyed by the product by the reflection of the Brand's Values. For example, if the brand values are environmentally friendly, natural, high quality, then a duvet cover in 100% unbleached organic Egyptian cotton (with polished coconut husk buttons) will reflect the brand values and reinforce the use of the brand. Such use of brand values must also be consistent in order to be effective, otherwise the subtlety of the message will be wasted. It therefore makes sense to consider these brand values when developing or sourcing products, to ensure that they are included from the outset and that time is not wasted on products which will ultimately prove unsuitable.

Brand values should be included in the decision process when building the product range.

Communication Through Packaging

The type of packaging selected, its style and graphics, should again reflect the brand values. It is easy to become over-sophisticated or complicated with packaging, whereas simplicity can convey the brand value in a much clearer way to the customer, and help the image to remain consistent. If a myriad permutations exist for the use of the brand on graphics, then inconsistencies will inevitably arise and the value of the brand will be diluted.

Packaging is often taken to be a box or container, but many products are sold loose on the shelves. "Packaging" in these instances can include swing labels, the price ticket or product information tags. Attention to detail in these areas can be vital in the reinforcement of the brand. What would a lop-sided, dog-eared price ticket convey about your brand?

Communication Through Promotion

The communication of the brand is not restricted just to the product and its packaging. It extends to all forms of communication such as adverts, press releases and promotional material. The use of the brand should remain consistent across the different media in order to reinforce its identity and integrity.

6. Managing the Brand

The establishing of a brand can take many years. Think how long some of the most famous brands, such as Coca Cola or Castrol have been around. Years of investment have gone into their creation and it is vital that the brand is properly managed on an ongoing basis in order to retain its market awareness.

 Management of the brand is crucial in order to retain its integrity and success.

The first stage in this management process should be a brand audit to assess what the current position is and to identify the key areas to address. So how do you conduct a brand audit?

Case Example

There is no one exclusive method, but the following table provides a guide to an approach. The table has been completed for a fictitious clothing retailer called "Traders".

The brand audit for "Traders Ltd" identified the following points which will require action if the brand is to retain and develop credibility.

• The products which do not reflect the brand values should be amended or discontinued.

• The typeface for the brand should be standardised.

• The number of sizes of the logo should be reduced to a more manageable number.

• The colours of the brand logo should be standardised.

• The brand logo should be introduced onto point of sale material.

• A policy should be developed for the consistent positioning of the brand logo throughout the business.

BRAND AUDIT

Company name: *Traders Ltd*

Brand Name: *Traders Ltd*

Brand Core Values: *Ethnic, Fair Trade, Value For Money*

Brand Secondary Values: *Vibrant, Integrity*

PRODUCT REVIEW

Total number of products: *520*

Number of products which incorporate brand values: *467*

Number of products which don't incorporate brand values: *53*

BRAND USAGE REVIEW

	Product	packaging	POS (Shelf hangers/ Price tags)	Marketing (Promotions/ Adverts)
Typeface	*Times Roman*	*Times Arial*	*Arial*	*Arial*
Size	*2/10 cm*	*10/20 cm*	*10/15/30 cm*	*5/15 cm*
Colour	*red/yellow*	*red/yellow orange/yellow*	*orange/red*	*blue/yellow*
Style	*oval*	*square*	*oval square*	*rectangle*
Positioning	*Neck label Arm Breast pocket*	*Box Lg carrier*	*None*	*Central Top RHS LHS*

Assignment 8:3 Brand Audit

Using the blank version of the brand audit form (below), undertake a brand audit on your brand or company.

Draw up a list of action points which would rectify misuse or inconsistent use of the brand.

BRAND AUDIT

Company name:

Brand Name:

Brand Core Values:

Brand Secondary Values:

PRODUCT REVIEW

Total number of products:

Number of products which incorporate brand values:

Number of products which don't incorporate brand values:

BRAND USAGE REVIEW

	Product	packaging	POS (Shelf hangers/ Price tags)	Marketing (Promotions/ Adverts)
Typeface				
Size				
Colour				
Style				
Positioning				

7. Brand Extensions

Once a business has developed a brand which is successful, a search is frequently made for extensions into other product areas. For example, a retailer of branded notebooks may decide to extend the brand into other stationery products, or within other product areas. A large number of designer clothing retailers are now looking to extend the brand into homewares. However such diverse brand extensions are not always sensible for the business.

In order for a brand extension to be successful, it needs to appear logical to the consumer and be able to transfer the same brand values onto the product range. For example, if Heinz were to start selling shoes it would appear incongruous with their brand identity, but Marlborough were able to extend the brand to clothing because of the strong lifestyle associations linked with the brand. "Marlborough Man" had been seen in check shirt and jeans for years, smoking his cigarette, so why shouldn't the customer buy the clothes as well as the cigarettes?

8. Summary

In this chapter we have considered:

- what makes a brand
- its key benefits to the retailer
- how the brand can be communicated to the customer and, finally
- how the brand can be managed to ensure that it retains its integrity and its benefits to the business.

This chapter concludes the section of the book on developing the product range. In the next section we will consider the selling of the product, the monitoring of performance and the presentation of the product in-store.

Checklist

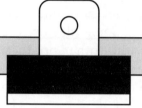

1. A brand should have a unique identity which is easily recognised by the customer.

2. Brands help to generate sales revenue when they are clearly defined and targeted at specific customers.

3. The development of a brand can allow for higher margins to be achieved.

4. Brands can generate customer loyalty but loyalty is built on trust. If the trust is broken then so is customer loyalty.

5. Brand values have to be valued by the customer or they will fail to generate the anticipated product sales.

6. Brand values should be included in the decision process when building the product range.

7. Management of the brand is crucial in order to retain its integrity and success.

PART THREE

IMPLEMENTATION

"Buying is both an art and a science. The art is to put into practice what the science tells you. The science is to review constantly what you achieve."

Stephen Shooman
Director of Merchandising
Allders Department Stores

9

Performance Review

1. Introduction

After all the planning, product selection and buying, when the trading period actually begins, the main focus will be on the question "How are we doing?" In reality, performance review is a constant process, as is buying, but it is probably helpful for us to think of it in isolation in order to fully understand its importance. Performance review is not only important for the business, to compare its results to the budget, but it is also important for the individual buyer who needs to know how well they are doing, personally, in the job. This chapter deals with both aspects of performance review.

Starting with sales review, we will identify the other key performance factors that should be included. We will also consider the issue of performance reporting:

Who gets what information and how often?

We will define a structured approach to solving sales (and other) trading problems and take a look at forecasting methods and techniques. Finally we will look at stock issues, by examining stock commitment and intake, and considering risk as it applies to stock investment.

2. The Purpose of Review

Why should we review our performance?

- It is needed to compare current trading performance to the planned levels set out in the buying budget.
- It is needed to assess individual buyer performance.

But, why is it important?

Performance review would be pointless if it failed to prompt some kind of action appropriate to the current trading situation. Where performance is below the required level, a review should prompt action that will put the business back on course to achieve, as a minimum, the level of gross profit expressed in the buying budget. Where performance is exceeding targeted levels, the review should prompt action that will support and sustain current levels of achievement.

Businesses will often conduct a post mortem review after important promotional events or trading periods like a main Sale, Events or Christmas. This will involve an analysis of what happened, the identification of areas for improvement and a review of lessons learnt will take place. Or, put simply:

- What did we achieve? (the results review)
- What could we have done better?
- What have we learnt?
- What will we do differently as a result of this review?

The aim should be to learn from the experience and improve performance in a similar event or promotion, next time round.

 The main reason for conducting a critical review of current trading performance is to take immediate action for short-term gain, and apply what has been learnt to benefit the business in the longer term.

The buyer undoubtedly has a major role in the achievement of the buying budget in all its aspects. Whilst it is true that the achievement of the sales budget, for example, cannot be solely the responsibility of any one person, it is the buyer who has a major influence on the result. To what extent the buyer is actually held accountable for the achievement of the levels of performance contained within the buying budget will depend on the culture and structure of the organisation, as discussed in Chapter 2.

If the organisation is one that embodies the concept of accountability within its management culture, the buyer, along with other managers and staff, will be clear about and fully aware of their specific goals and objectives. Furthermore, the buyer will expect to have his/her performance measured against those specified objectives and be held accountable for the results.

 Good performance may be rewarded by management simply acknowledging the achievement or it may be recognised more formally, through some kind of incentive bonus scheme.

Poor trading performance will usually be the result of a combination of factors: internal and external. These factors need to be thoroughly examined in order to identify the real source of the problem, or problems. It is only when problems have been clearly identified, that we can hope to solve them! Buying is not an exact science. We all make mistakes. The question, when it comes to buyer performance is:

When does failure to achieve the required result become a disqualifying weakness?

Case History

The Edgar's Department Store Group in South Africa supports the view that crimes of omission should be treated more seriously than crimes of commission. In other words, failure to act is viewed more seriously than taking action that subsequently proves to be ineffective.

We take actions based on our best judgement at the time. There are no guarantees of success. It is easy to be wise after the event. In a product sell-out situation, which view would your buying manager take?

"Well done – we sold all the product at full price without incurring any markdown," or
"You should have bought more!"

3. The Review Process

Performance review will happen informally, all the time in a retail organisation, but there will usually be some more formal reviews that take place weekly and/or monthly. These reviews will tend to be conducted in meetings between the buyers and buying managers. Where a merchandising function exists, then merchandisers and their managers will also be involved.

Performance review will normally involve reviewing sales, and other key performance factors – stockturn, planned margin, achieved margin, gross profit and perhaps, sales density looking at this year's results compared to last year's results and plan, quoting variances expressed either in percentage or value terms, or both.

Actual performance will fall into one of 3 categories:

- above plan
- on plan
- below plan.

For our purposes here, we will focus on results comparison against the levels of performance required by the buying budget that we will refer to as the plan. If the goal is to achieve the results contained in the plan, then reviewing performance against the plan must be more relevant than comparing performance to the previous year.

Where sales are on target, a review will provide the check that reassures us that no exceptional intervention is required. It is where sales are above or below plan that intervention of some kind will be needed. In either case, it is important to understand why our actual results are at variance with the plan. It can often be something of a mystery. Until we can understand why the results are as they are, it will be impossible to know what to do to bring performance back on course.

The performance report will show you what has happened in the business, e.g. that sales are below plan by 5%, gross profit is 8% below plan, stock is 10% above plan etc. What it will not be able to tell you is why?

 The buyer needs to take a magnifying glass to the results contained in the performance report to find out where the problems are.

We need to adopt an investigative approach. In solving a crime, a detective will follow a structured approach involving a 3-step investigative process – information gathering and review, drawing conclusions based on the facts and finally, having identified the guilty party, making the arrest!

The buyer can learn from this approach and, with some minor amendments, apply it to the retail situation!

Let's see how this could work…

Step 1 – Investigation

- Review the results.
- Seek comment/input from those with informed opinions to improve your understanding of why the results are what they are.

Step 2 – Draw Conclusions

- Identify the key issues/problems.
- Weigh up alternative solutions.
- Identify an action plan.

Step 3 – Implement!

- Define who will take what action, and by when.
- Follow up to ensure that the actions are taken.

Without this final step – the follow up – the review can have no guaranteed business impact.

4. Sales Review

It goes without saying that sales are a critical success factor for any retail business. Sales will always be the first performance factor to be reviewed, and it is sales that will tend to be most frequently reviewed. Sales are closely monitored at every level in the business from product line level to overall department level, and every level in between, according to the structure of the business.

When conducting a critical review of sales, it is often useful to look at the sales trend, which can be demonstrated by using *Moving Annual Totals*. These strip out the seasonal factors, showing how year-on-year annual sales are increasing or declining. The trend thus exposed can be extrapolated to give a view of the future. An example is set out overleaf. The first chart shows the seasonal and promotional sales pattern. The second chart shows the moving annual total sales, revealing a clear upward trend over the last year.

Cookware Weekly Sales

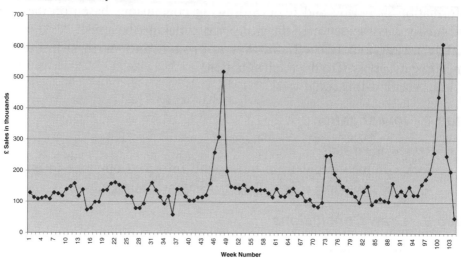

Cookware Sales Trend

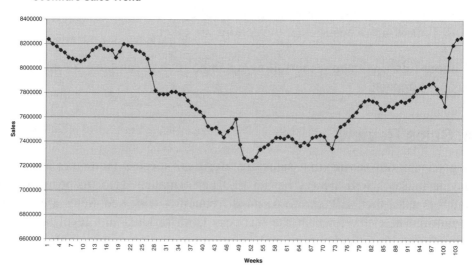

A moving annual total (MAT) is calculated by taking, at the end of each week, the sum of the previous 52 weeks. For example, in Week 52, MAT sales would be the sum of weeks 1 to 52. In Week 1, MAT sales would be the sales from week 2 last year to week 1 this year inclusive, and so on. Each week's calculation will drop out the "oldest" week and add on the latest reported result.

In retailing there is a phrase "Everything starts and ends with sales".

We start with sales when planning the budget and, in the final analysis, the measurement of successful buying activity is whether or not the product sells! In a situation of poor sales performance, how can we find out where the problems are? There will invariably be more than one problem causing poor sales performance, so it is important to be thorough in our approach.

What we need is a structured approach to problem solving, to ensure that we look in all the right places.

Consider the 5 Ps – Product, Price, Promotion, Place, and People.

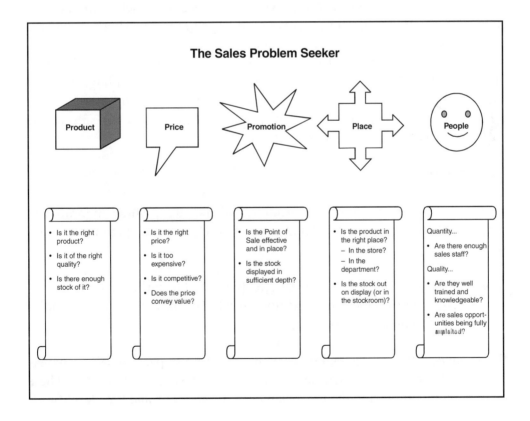

The Sales Problem Seeker

Product	Price	Promotion	Place	People
• Is it the right product? • Is it of the right quality? • Is there enough stock of it?	• Is it the right price? • Is it too expensive? • Is it competitive? • Does the price convey value?	• Is the Point of Sale effective and in place? • Is the stock displayed in sufficient depth?	• Is the product in the right place? – In the store? – In the department? • Is the stock out on display (or in the stockroom)?	Quantity... • Are there enough sales staff? Quality... • Are they well trained and knowledgeable? • Are sales opportunities being fully exploited?

Product

 The buyer's responsibility is to buy the right product, at the right price, in the right quantity, at the right time.

This is an old saying that has withstood the test of time. It neatly sums up the role of the buyer and encompasses 2 of our 5 Ps – product and price. Taking "product" first of all, what is the right product? The right product is one that customers will want to buy! If the product is right, there will be an irresistible desire to possess it. It will be aesthetically pleasing; it will meet the customers' needs and/or desires.

Price

What is the right price for the product? Whilst it is true that the buyer fixes the selling price, it is the customer who finally decides whether the price is right. There will be a certain expectation of price in the customer's mind, and a certain, subjective appreciation of value.

The right price will meet the customer's expectation of value. "The first price is always the best " is a policy upheld by many in retailing, but only successfully practised by a few. This is the concept of selling most of your product at the full (and first) price at which it is offered for sale to the customer. It is a concept of price integrity.

Promotion

This covers the strength of the promotional message, which incorporates point of sale material and its effectiveness. It also relates to operational issues such as:

- has the product been displayed effectively and in sufficient depth?
- was the promotional method appropriate for the type of merchandise being promoted?

For instance, 10% off ladies knitwear may have no impact on sales whereas 10% off electrical goods will be effective in increasing sales volume. There is more on this subject in the next chapter on Promotions and Profitability.

Place

Place refers to the location of the product within the department and even within the store. What is it that estate agents say are the 3 most important factors influencing the value of a property? Location, location and location! When determining the location of product within a store, we need to consider whether it is a "planned purchase" or an "impulse buy". For example, fashion accessories are often an "impulse buy" – not a pre-planned purchase, but something that the customer finds attractive and desirable, and decides to buy on the spur of the moment.

By contrast, coats are a planned purchase. They have a much higher price tag! The customer would normally plan to make such a purchase, and is more likely to shop around first before making a buying decision. So how does this impact on the ideal location of the product in the store? It is likely that customers will be prepared to seek out product that represents a "planned purchase" which could therefore be positioned at the back of the store, in a single floor shopping environment. An "impulse buy" product needs to be located in an area of high customer traffic flow, so that as many prospective customers as possible will see it. Remember that this is the product that customers may not be specifically looking for, but may want to buy, if they see it! Take a look at the sample ladieswear sales floor layout shown opposite; notice the location of the various product areas in relation to the main doors and customer walkways.

All product areas can be classified into 4 categories:

- planned purchases, e.g. lingerie, rainwear
- impulse buys, e.g. scarves
- distress purchases, e.g. umbrellas
- mixed, e.g. leisurewear, separates.

Ladieswear Sales Floor Layout

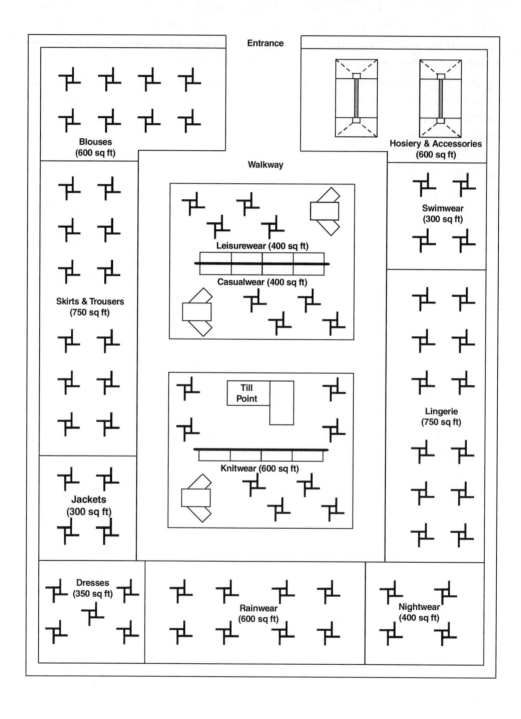

People

People issues cover the 2 dimensions of quantity and quality. Are there sufficient numbers of sales staff covering the product area? Are they of the right quality? Are they equipped to sell the product? That is, have they received appropriate and adequate training?

Raising questions under the 5 categories of product, price, promotion, place and people should provide the necessary answers to enable the formulation of solutions.

Assignment 9:1 Problem solving

Take an under-performing product area within your business and apply our structured approach to problem solving to help to locate specifically where the problems are.

Use the "Sales Problem-Seeker" (page 149) to ensure nothing is missed.

This structured approach to problem solving provides a method we can use, but in each of the 5 areas, there will be a need to dig more deeply, beyond the surface issues, to find the real problems.

We now have a method of approach that we can broadly apply to trading performance problems.

5. Other Key Performance Factors

Apart from sales, which we have identified as critically important, what other key performance factors should we review, and what can we do about problems in these areas?

Stockturn

Stockturn is really an expression that defines stock productivity. If the rate of stockturn is lower than the planned rate, then either we have too much stock or not enough sales, or more likely, a mixture of both! When sales fail to reach planned levels, the sales forecast will normally be reduced, and this will automatically increase the forward weeks cover that your stock represents. It is a simple and inescapable fact, that when sales go down, stock in weeks cover goes up!

The See-saw Effect

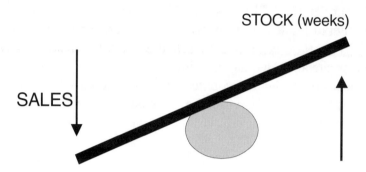

The implications of a slower than planned rate of stockturn can be serious.

- Lower than expected sales will cause higher stocks than planned.
- Being overstocked reduces Open to buy.
- Reduced open to buy will restrict the intake of new stock into the business.
- Reduced stock intake may dilute the planned margin and have an adverse impact on sales.

It is easy to see the start of a negative spiral that will lead to a downward sales trend that could become increasingly difficult to reverse.

How can such a situation be tackled? Reversing the sales trend would resolve the stock problem. We can begin to see the power of the "everything starts and ends with sales" statement. However, it may be necessary to take action to reduce stock levels as well. This could be achieved by marking down some currently held stock, or by postponing or cancelling forward commitments. Possible actions on stock are discussed in more detail under the heading of "stocks" later in this chapter.

Planned Margin

Planned margin, as we have seen, is the margin at which goods are brought into the business. This margin would translate into gross profit if we sold all our goods at full price without any markdowns! If the margin on stock intake is lower than the budgeted requirement, then there are two main possibilities:

1) The buyer has failed to secure the right buying price to generate the required planned margin at the selling prices that have been set
2) The stock entering the business is showing a lower collective average than the budget requires. In other words it's in the mix.

Markdowns and Achieved Margin

Performance reports will show actual markdowns taken to date. These will usually be shown with their variance from last year and variance from this year's plan. These factual results cannot be altered. What can be adjusted however, is the markdown forecast for the remainder of the trading period.

Unlike sales performance, which can, at best, be influenced, markdowns can be controlled and can thereby be used as a tool to manage the margin. We should consider markdowns in two categories: promotional and clearance. Planned promotional markdowns are those which are designed to have a predicted impact on sales, achieved margin and thereby, gross profit. There will be more on this subject in our next chapter. Whilst there will probably be some provision for them, clearance markdowns represent failure.

Clearance markdowns will be applied to products that, for whatever reason, have failed to attract the customer.

The product was not sufficiently desirable, at least, not at that price. Price is a key factor, a trigger that can switch a product from being a slow seller to a fast seller overnight! Price can turn a "dog" into a "star'!

Whilst markdowns reduce the achieved margin, they can also influence sales. If sales can be sufficiently increased then the gross profit can be improved. Markdowns are certainly a key performance factor, which impact directly on the gross profit result.

Gross Profit

Gross profit pays the wages! This statement has a wonderful tendency to focus the thinking.

Budgeted gross profit can be achieved by having relatively high sales at a low margin or conversely, low sales at a high margin; the end result is the same. The chosen route for a retail business will be determined within its buying policy. At buyer level, there is much more flexibility, and sales response to buying activity will, in part, determine the path to be taken. As we have seen, it is clearance markdowns that pose the biggest threat to the margin.

However, it is the achievement of the gross profit target that is critically important to the business.

Gross profit is the single most important budgetary target the buyer must aim to hit!

As such, the gross profit result is one that is most keenly anticipated.

It is therefore, of interest to the buyer, and all managers in the business, to know exactly how well the business is performing and, in particular, how well their part of it is doing! The way this information is conveyed is the subject of our next section.

6. Performance Reporting

When you ask people in various retail organisations what they think of their performance reporting, you will typically get answers like this:

"There's just too much information, I don't have time to read it all"
"A lot of it isn't relevant to me, I just look at it and throw it in the bin"

At different levels within any organisation, different information is needed. The level of detail increases as you move down through the management structure.

Smart businesses recognise their information needs and treat their management as customers of their management reports. Once this concept of "internal customers" is acknowledged, the idea of assessing specific reporting needs becomes a natural and obvious thing to do.

Step 1 – Find out what your customers want and how often they want it.
Step 2 – Fulfil their needs in the most efficient way.

When it comes to performance reporting, it's easy to produce too much of the wrong information and distribute it too frequently to the wrong people!

One way to measure the effectiveness of performance reports is to ask the recipients what they do with them. Or, to put it another way, how does the report influence their actions to improve the business?

Assignment 9:2 *Reports analysis*

List the reports you receive on the checklist supplied below and against each one show the frequency of issue, e.g. weekly, monthly etc. Then against each entry show what you do as a direct result of receiving that report.

Performance Report Checklist

Report details:		Description of contents	Issue frequency	Action on receipt?
Document name	Doc Ref No			

What about the content of these reports – what should they include?

At product section level and above, the key performance factors that need to be included are:

Sales – for the period (weekly or 4 weekly), with the variance against last year and plan. Cumulative sales (year to date) should also be included with the same comparisons to last year and plan,

Stocks – closing stock for the period, with the variance against last year and plan quoted in value terms and representative week's sales cover.

Planned margin – margin rate compared to last year and plan, both for the period and cumulatively.

Achieved margin – margin rate compared to last year and plan, for the period and cumulatively.

Gross profit – the value of gross profit achieved this year compared to last year and plan with variances shown for the period and cumulatively.

Markdowns – markdowns for the period and cumulatively compared to last year and plan. Performance reports typically look back on actual results, but some may be forward-looking and incorporate forecasts.

7. Sales forecasting

One of the key outcomes of any performance review process is a realistic sales forecast.

Having reviewed actual performance to date, it should be possible to provide a more accurate view of the future than that contained in the original buying budget. We have seen how Open to buy is created in Chapter 4 "Planning the Budget", but once the trading period has begun, it is the sales forecast that should drive the Open to buy.

An over-optimistic sales forecast will generate more Open to buy and therefore expose the business to greater risk through excessive stock investment. Conversely, a pessimistic sales forecast may impede sales growth by restricting stock intake, unless stockturn is better than plan.

A good sales forecast provides a realistic view of the future by taking into account all known factors that will affect the business.

What methods and techniques are used to forecast sales?

A crystal ball is one option! There are, however, some other, more scientific methods we can consider. One such method is the "straight line" forecast, which assumes that current performance as reflected in the cumulative variance against plan, will continue.

An example is set out below.

Example

If sales are cumulatively 18% up against the plan, a straight-line forecast will project sales to the end of the trading period to show an 18% surplus against plan.

Straight-line Sales Forecast

Towel Sales	Year to date	Balance	Full year
Planned Sales	186,000	1,289,000	1,475,000
Actual Sales Actual v Plan	219,480 18.0%		
Forecast Sales Forecast v Plan		1,521,000 18.0%	
Actual+Forecast Sales Actual+Forecast v Plan			1,740,500 18.0%

Typically, where this method is used, it is as a "base", a starting point. The next step would be to apply any other known factors that are likely to affect the sales trend, typically in the short term – things like planned promotional activity. Where promotions have been added since the formulation of the plan, it would be appropriate to evaluate their impact on sales and feed that impact into the sales forecast.

What is different now that justifies a revised view of the future?

What actions will be taken that will alter the present sales trend and what impact will those actions have on sales? These are questions that need to be answered if the sales forecast is to be amended.

However the sales forecast is derived, a word of caution – over optimism is almost endemic in retailing!

 The value of the open to buy as a management tool for controlling the business and its investment in stock relies heavily on the accuracy of the sales forecast.

The greater the period covered by the sales forecast the greater the potential for inaccuracy.

8. Gross Profit Forecasting

The gross profit forecast is derived from a combination of the sales forecast and the achieved margin forecast. The key difference between forecasting sales and forecasting gross profit is that sales can, at best, be influenced, but the gross profit can be controlled, at least to a certain extent, through the control of intake margin (planned margin) and markdowns.

The important issue here is will the gross profit target be met? A realistic and early view of the period-end gross profit result, even if frightening, will give the opportunity to review strategy and make course corrections if the business is not on track to achieve its targeted objectives. Forewarned is forearmed!

9. Stock Commitment and Intake

Stock can be divided up into three categories that describe its status:

- stock held within the business
- stock ordered but not yet received (commitment)
- open to buy – money available for future investment in stock.

Being understocked is easily resolved – spend the open to buy, buy more stock!

This is not usually a problem for the buyer! Being overstocked is, however, more of a problem and it can be tackled in a number of ways:

- Find a sales solution; improve promotion of the product in store through better location, a bigger display or, better, more eye-catching point of sale material.
- Add value to the product in some way, e.g. offer a "gift with purchase" consumer incentive.
- In a multiple outlet retail organisation, transfer it to a better location where it will sell faster. Not all stores will sell a product at the same rate.
- Ask the supplier to take some stock back.
- Apply a markdown, which will immediately reduce the value of the stock (at retail) and will also, hopefully, increase sales.

If all else fails – if it's a "dog" – mark it down. Clear it out. Start again. You will then have the open to buy to re-invest in new product lines.

 Hoarding slow selling stock in the hope of avoiding a markdown, is a recipe for disaster!

It ties up open to buy, preventing investment in new stock. Stock will never sell from the stockroom if it is removed from sale and, unlike a fine wine, it will not improve with age, it will only deteriorate! The only sensible solution is to sell it, at whatever price the customer is prepared to pay for it.

Commitment is the term used to describe stock that has been ordered from the supplier, but has not yet been delivered. What can be done about this category of stock in an overstocked situation? Postponing delivery may be appropriate, or even order cancellation may be necessary, depending on the severity of the stock position. However, it should be remembered that an order constitutes a contract with the supplier. Do you really want to break that contract? Are you prepared to do it with or without the supplier's agreement?

Cancellation of orders could permanently sour the business relationship with your supplier. You have to weigh up whether that is a price worth paying!

Open to buy is our final stock category. It is really "potential stock" in that it is money available for stock investment. An "overbought" situation can be created either by a sales shortfall against the plan, or simply by overspending. If we liken the open to buy to a household budget, it's like being overdrawn at the bank! If you have an overdraft, you have effectively committed some of your future income. In an overstocked, overbought situation, you have spent some of your forward open to buy allowance. In both cases, this creates a buying restriction in the short to medium-term and is certainly not ideal. Timescales are important here. In some product areas, notably in clothing, commitment takes place some months in advance of the selling season. As we saw in the earlier section on forecasting, the further ahead into the future the forecast extends, the greater the likelihood of inaccuracy. Short-term forecasts are easier to get right! With extended buying lead times as applicable to clothing products, the risk increases. Stock may be bought to support a sales plan that is subsequently reduced, creating an overstocked position even before the season starts.

10. Summary

In this chapter on performance review, we have questioned the need for review and considered the potential benefits of effective review in terms of the benefits both to the business and the individual buyer's performance.

We have considered a structured approach to problem solving that has a practical application in day to day buying activity. This encourages a "dig deeper" investigative approach to discover where the real problems lie, essential if we are to come up with the right solutions.

We have also identified what performance factors need to be reported and have given some consideration to what we can do about adverse performance, by reviewing some possible courses of action. Sales forecasting is central to the review process since so much depends on it, including the open to buy and the period end gross profit forecast. Our section on stocks has highlighted the dangers of over-commitment to stock and the risk to which it exposes us. Performance review is about looking back, reacting to trading results, learning what we can from the experience, and putting that knowledge to good use in the future.

Our ability to steer the business on its desired course will depend on the utilisation of a number of resources and skills. We have already examined the importance of sales forecasting which forms the basis of our gross profit forecast. But, managing a retail business is not just about review and reaction, we need to be visionary, proactive and be able to take the initiative. One of the main weapons in our armoury is our promotional proposition. When and how we promote our merchandise will impact heavily on our sales results and profitability. Our next chapter looks at the whole issue of promotions and profitability.

Checklist

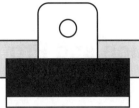

1. The main reason for conducting a critical review of current trading performance is to take immediate action for short-term gain, and apply what has been learnt to benefit the business in the longer term.

2. Good performance may be rewarded by management acknowledging the achievement or, it may be recognised more formally, through some kind of incentive bonus scheme

3. The buyer needs to take a magnifying glass to the results contained in the performance report to find out where the problems are.

4. In retailing there is a phrase "Everything starts and ends with sales"

5. The buyer's responsibility is to buy the right product, at the right price, in the right quantity, at the right time.

6. Clearance markdowns will be applied to products that, for whatever reason, have failed to attract the customer.

7. Gross profit is the single most important budgetary target the buyer must aim to hit!

8. When it comes to performance reporting, it's easy to produce too much of the wrong information and distribute it too frequently to the wrong people!

9. A good sales forecast provides a realistic view of the future by taking all known factors that will affect the business, into account.

10. The value of the open to buy as a management tool for controlling the business and its investment in stock relies heavily on the accuracy of the sales forecast.

11. Hoarding slow selling stock in the hope of avoiding a markdown is a recipe for disaster!

10

Promotion and Profitability

1. Introduction

When we think of the idea of promotion, the word "Sale" no doubt springs readily to mind! But promotional activity can take many different forms, as we will explore in this chapter. The section devoted to promotional methods lists the main types of promotion available and attempts to link them to promotional objectives. Whilst outline promotional activity can – and should – be planned in advance of the season, it is also important to be able to respond to current, in-season trading conditions with new initiatives.

We will consider these two types of promotion: pro-active and reactive and, in particular, focus on how buyers can shape and influence the promotional activity that affects the product group within their buying responsibility.

Promotions, like all business initiatives, should be carefully planned. Objectives should be clearly stated, so that the results can be reviewed against them allowing the question "Was it worth it?" to be satisfactorily answered.

Reviewing the success of promotional activity not only has direct, immediate relevance to the current trading period, but also to the formulation of future promotional plans. If you ask a retailer why they are holding a particular promotional event, you might get the reply, *"Because we had one last year at this time!"* Whether the promotion was effective last year is quite another matter! It is easy to fall into "the promotion trap" of mounting promotions out of habit.

We should first consider why we have promotions. What are we hoping to achieve by them?

2. Aims and Objectives

It is important to define the objectives of any planned promotional activity so that we can effectively measure the results!

Let's consider some of the most common promotional objectives:

- increase sales and gross profit
- increase customer traffic
- clear stock
- establish brand, or product awareness
- establish retailer excellence.

Promotions will usually have one or more of these objectives. Let's examine each one more closely.

a) Increasing Sales and Gross Profit

To sell more and make more gross profit – this must be the most common promotional objective. The "selling more" piece is relatively easy to achieve, whilst the "make more gross profit" part is often much more difficult and illusive!

To increase sales you could develop a promotional strategy to:

- increase the average transaction value, (the average spend per customer) or,
- increase the number of transactions (the number of customers coming into the store and making a purchase) or,
- there is a whole host of promotional activities aimed at doing either of these – or both!

We will consider some of the alternative promotional methods in the next section of this chapter. But first, let's consider this promotional objective, to increase sales and gross profit, in more detail.

To sell *more* you could reduce the retail price of the product. This assumes, of course, that the product is price-sensitive and that you will sell more if you reduce the price. To make more gross profit, you would have to increase the units sold by a sufficient percentage to compensate for any reduction in achieved margin.

Gross Profit Break-even Point

Product X	Selling price	Cost price	Profit per unit	Margin %	Sales in Units	Gross Profit
Alternative Price A	16.99	7.49	9.50	55.9	2,368	22,500
Normal Selling Price	**14.99**	**7.49**	**7.50**	**50.0**	**3,000**	**22,500**
Alternative Price B	12.99	7.49	5.50	42.3	4,091	22,500

In this example, increasing the selling price by £2 would mean that only 2,368 units would have to be sold to realise the same gross profit as at the "normal" selling price of £14.99. If the selling price were reduced by £2 to £12.99, volume sales would have to increase by 1,091 units or 36% to realise the gross profit amount.

It is all too easy to gain additional sales volume but lose overall gross profit.

 Beware of the "busy fools" syndrome; reducing the selling price may cause everyone to work harder and sell more, but for no extra profit!

Remember, there may be additional costs associated with price reductions e.g. advertising or point of sale costs, that could reduce profitability even further.

However, a reduction in retail price may not always be accompanied by a reduction in achieved margin. The cost to the margin may be borne in whole, or in part by the supplier providing a reduction in the cost price. In these circumstances, it is easier for the retailer to make more gross profit, since there is a lower volume sales requirement to break-even.

b) Increasing Customer Traffic

Customers entering a retail outlet are often referred to as "customer footfall", or "customer traffic". Traffic-builder promotions provide a way of increasing customer traffic flow.

In the last section we identified two promotional strategies for driving up sales volumes:

- increasing the average transaction value
- increasing the number of transactions.

If the aim is to increase the number of transactions or, put another way, the number of customers entering your store who actually make a purchase, then it is necessary to consider what stimulates people to come shopping in the first place! What prompts a purchase?

All purchases can be broadly categorised into:

- *Impulse buys*
  These are the products you didn't know you were going to buy! They have immediate appeal and are often easy purchasing decisions.
- *Planned purchases*
  These are often larger, higher priced items that are well-considered purchases. They are products for which the consumer is more prepared to "shop around".
- *Distress purchases*
  These are the purchases that we are forced into making because something has broken, worn out, or failed in some way and we need to replace it. It may not be something we want to buy, but we feel we have to!

 If we can understand what inspires the customer to make a purchase, it should be easier to identify the type of promotion most likely to get the best sales results.

Assignment 10:1 Purchase types

Against each of the following products, tick the boxes to indicate the type of purchase the product is most likely to represent.

Product	Impulse Buy	Planned Purchase	Distress Purchase
Washine machine			
Tights			
Nappies			
Coat			
Dress			
Umbrella			
Suitcase			
Vacuum cleaner			
Car			
Towels			
Sofa bed			
Rug			
TV			

One way to increase customer traffic flow is by the creation of a "loss leader" product. This is a product where the achieved margin is unacceptably low by normal standards, but is justified by the consumer interest it will attract. The gross profit on a specific product may be sacrificed to increase customer traffic flow. It will often be a case of short-term loss for longer-term gain.

Apart from the direct sales response to the promoted product itself, there will be a beneficial spin-off effect for the impulse-buy-product in any "traffic-builder" promotions.

c) Clearance

Even in the best run retail organisations there will always be a need to clear stocks of old, unseasonal or unsuccessful product. The end of season Sale was originally conceived as a mechanism for clearing current season's stock before the new season's stock arrived. The Sale, as we know it today, is also used as an opportunity to promote special purchases – high volume buys designed to exploit the sales opportunity presented to the retailer by increased customer footfall at Sale-time.

When to clear seasonal stock can be a difficult decision governed partly by the weather, partly by what competitors are doing and partly by the needs of the business in clearing out the old stock to make way for the new.

The "unsuccessful buy", is the product that just did not sufficiently impress the customer or, at least, in sufficient quantity to sell through. Whilst this stock remains unsold, it is tying up open to buy that could otherwise be invested in new stock with, arguably, a better chance of selling.

Old stock is a thorny issue. It is product that is likely to have been marked down, but has nevertheless failed to sell.

The best thing to do with old stock is to get rid of it! Old stock ties up the open to buy in the same way as the unsuccessful buy.

d) Establishing Brand Awareness

When launching or re-launching a brand or product, introductory offers will often be used to encourage customer trial. Similarly, when seeking to build brand awareness for a newly launched brand or product, money saving offers can be used to great effect. Multi-buy and save offers are useful here too; they encourage customer familiarity with the product and thereby encourage brand loyalty.

New product promotion is about selling the features and benefits of the product and is not always accompanied by a consumer price incentive!

e) Establishing Excellence

Store loyalty cards are now a very familiar part of the retail scene. Having a strong, loyal customer base is an asset for any retailer when all are having to work harder to maintain market share. There is often a perceived need by the retailer to establish or enhance their reputation in some specific area of product or service. In almost every market sector there are brand leaders. In the retail sector, there are retailers whose product specialism makes them a first choice destination for shoppers, e.g. Marks & Spencer for underwear.

They may already be established as a "centre of excellence" or may wish to enhance their credibility in a specific product area. This may be achieved through a variety of promotional initiatives designed to increase market share in a specific product sector.

To become the customers' first choice destination the retailer may need a sustained promotional drive supported by strong advertising support in addition to excellent product ranges.

3. Promotional Methods

In this section we consider the various promotional methods we have at our disposal to help us achieve the promotional aims and objectives we have defined.

Let's look at some of these promotional methods that are primarily aimed at influencing sales by affecting the real or perceived value of the product:

- *Money off*
  Direct price discounting. The price is promoted using phrases like "20% off" or, "£20 off" Here, the retailer is reliant on attracting more customers, increasing the number of transactions.

- *Multi-buy and save*
  The individual product price is reduced when two or more products are purchased together in a multi-buy. This raises the average transaction value, increasing the customer spend, and at the same time gives the customer better value for money.

- *Free Offers: Buy two, get one Free*
  In this offer, the customer will get better value for money by getting more of the product for the same price. This should increase the number of transactions.

- *Extended credit*
  The "buy now, pay later" option may appeal to the customer where parting with a lump sum in full payment is undesirable. They can have the benefit of using the product by paying for it as they use it. There may be a deposit required from the customer and a choice of period over which the balance is to be paid. There is, of course, an interest charge paid by the customer for extended credit.

- *Interest free credit (IFC)*
  This is a popular variation on the "buy now, pay later" principle, where the interest is not directly charged to the customer, and the retailer bears the cost of financing the loan.

  Both "Extended Credit" and "Interest Free" are used for large, usually planned purchases, e.g. furniture, carpets and large electrical goods.

- *Gift with purchase (GWP)*
  This is an indirect discount, in that you pay the normal price for the main product, but are receiving an extra item free. There is increased value for the customer, which drives up sales by increasing the number of transactions.

- *Purchase with purchase (PWP)*
  This provides the customer with an opportunity to buy something in addition to the main purchase, but at a reduced price. This increases the average spend per customer.

- *Money-off next purchase*
  To encourage customer loyalty, the first purchase of the product may or may not be discounted, but the offer of "money-off" the next purchase acts as an incentive for the customer to stay loyal to the product or brand.

- *Vouchers*
  The offer of gift vouchers provides the customer with a discount of a sort, in that the gift voucher gives a price reduction on the purchase of another product at some later date or time. This encourages a return visit to the store, benefiting the impulse buy product and helping to increase customer traffic. Vouchers give the customer a reason to come back.

- *A Chance to Win!*
  Competitions attract the gambler in everyone! They can add excitement to the retail experience. Depending on what is available to win and the perceived value of the prize, this type of promotion may draw in new customers, thereby increasing customer flow. This increased customer flow would be expected to result in higher sales by increasing the number of transactions.

- *Product in-store demonstration*

  A good demonstrator is a powerful sales aid! Product demonstration is a particularly useful technique where the point of sale and product packaging fail adequately to demonstrate the product features and benefits to the customer. More importantly, a good demonstrator, by attracting attention to the product, will not only increase the number of purchases, but also encourage a higher average transaction value through add-on sales.

- *Demonstration videos in-store*

  Often produced by suppliers of branded products, these promotional tools can be very successful in catching customers' attention. In-store videos can help to communicate messages which are too complex to fit onto a point of sale ticket, e.g. how to lay carpet tiles, or use a piece of multi-functional food preparation equipment for the kitchen! There is a danger, of course, if the video is particularly interesting, that the attracted crowd will simply block the customer walkways! Siting is an important operational consideration.

- *Product stack-piling*

  Sometimes referred to as "merchandise intimidation", a product presented in this way cannot fail to grab customers' attention, since they might otherwise fall over it! Combined with a strong price message, this can be a powerful promotional tool. It may be an old technique, but it is one that has never lost its impact – *"pile it high, sell it cheap!"*

- *Personal selling*

  Not to be under-estimated, personal selling still plays an important part in retailing in general, and in certain types of purchase in particular. Notably, "planned purchases" (which tend to involve higher priced items, which are bought less frequently) tend to be more considered purchases. There may also be additional, technical or other product information that the salesperson needs to provide for the customer in this situation.

A key sales opportunity presented by personal selling is the add-on (or related) sale; these are the extras that can often be sold as additional to the main purchase, thereby increasing the transaction value.

To re-cap on our review of promotions so far, we have considered:

- what we aim to achieve from our promotional activity – objectives set
- how we intend to achieve our objectives – promotional strategy planned
- why the customer makes a purchase – purchase motivation analysed
- which promotional methods we should select – types of promotion chosen.

Now try to put these four promotional elements together:

The following diagram takes the objective of increasing sales and gross profit and matches strategy, purchase motivation and types of promotion.

Matching Promotional Methods and Objectives

Purchase Motivation	Strategy:	
	Increased number of transactions	Increased average transaction value
	Types of Promotion	
Planned purchase	Money off Free offers IFC and Extended Credit GWP Vouchers A Chance to Win! Product demos and personal selling	IFC and Extended Credit Product demos and personal selling PWP
Impulse Buy	Money off Free offers GWP A Chance to Win! Product demos and personal selling Multi-buy and Save Money off next purchase Stack piling	Multi-buy and Save Product demos and personal selling PWP
Distress Purchase	Money off Free offers IFC and Extended Credit GWP Product demos and personal selling	Product demos and personal selling IFC and Extended Credit
	Methods	

Assignment 10:2 Objective matching

Repeat the exercise of matching objectives to methods, taking each of the remaining key objectives in turn:

• Increasing customer traffic

• Stock clearance

• Establishing brand, or product awareness

• Establishing retailer excellence

 In planning promotions: set objectives, define strategy, consider the motivation to purchase, select the promotional method and communicate it!

4. Promotional Support

The impact of any promotional message will depend on how well it is communicated.

Advertising and point of sale are the two major tools we have to communicate our product offer, its key features and value. Advertising can be generic – to build image: and product specific – to solicit customer response to a specific product or range of products. Point of sale material in-store can similarly be generic or product specific in nature. In larger organisations, the advertising and visual merchandising departments will have primary responsibility for the management of marketing activity. So what influence can the buyer have in these areas?

a) Advertising

The buyer is the main contact between the retailer and the supplier. The buyer should seek to exploit fully the opportunities for shared advertising and promotion – shared ideas and shared cost! For instance, suppliers of branded products will usually have an advertising budget, part of which is allocated to fund "shared cost" or contributory advertising with their customers.

The supplier can often help by supplying press releases for new products or product ranges. These press articles can be very powerful promotional tools, especially when linked to consumer incentives.

If a product is going to receive advertising support, there would logically be an expectation of increased sales volume in comparison with a period when no advertising support was given. Although this seems obvious, it is quite common for a promoted product to sell out – due to underestimation of the sales potential that advertising can provide. The reasons for this are numerous, but are often linked to rushed planning leading to unrealistic deadlines that cannot be met!

Measurement of the sales results of previous, similar advertising activity should give some guidance to the buyer on sales potential. The buyer obviously has a responsibility to provide adequate stock support for any promotional activity to ensure sales optimisation.

b) Point of Sale Material

Attractive point of sale material can draw the customer's attention to products that could otherwise be overlooked. The message does not always have to be "money-off".

Product-specific ticketing can successfully highlight a product to the customer, and act as a "silent salesperson". Ultimately, the effectiveness of point of sale material will depend on its visibility and the clarity of its message. Whilst buyers may not actually produce point of sale material, they do create the product range and are therefore ideally qualified to contribute ideas!

These ideas may be the buyers' own, or those formulated in conjunction with the supplier, the source being far less important than the outcome! In some market sectors, the supplier will actually provide point of sale material for the retailer.

 There is a huge opportunity for the buyer to achieve increased sales and gross profit by securing promotional support from suppliers, financial and conceptual!

5. Promotional Calendar

There will usually be an outline promotional plan created in advance of the trading season, produced in the form of a promotional calendar.

This schedules various types of promotion into various time-slots throughout the planning period. It describes what promotional activity will be happening and when, as illustrated in the sample promotional calendar shown here. In addition to the main events pre-planned by the retailer, there will, similarly, be pre-planned promotions that suppliers have initiated or that the buyers have created in conjunction with suppliers. The latter are often referred to as tailor-made promotions, and are very much a co-operative exercise.

Using a sample promotional calendar illustrated opposite, we can identify these different types of promotion:

- initiated by the retailer, e.g. Main and Mid-Season Sales
- initiated by the buyer, e.g. "Bed Month"
- initiated by the supplier, e.g. "Win a Car" Competition

Promotional Calendar

Promotional Activity	Period	Weeks
Winter Sale	1	1
Final Reductions	1	2
Spring Fashion	2	5–6
Great Value Lines	3	9–10
Easter Event	3	11
Mid Season Sale	4	13
Bed Month	4	14–15
Multi-buy and Save	5	17
Bank Holiday Specials	5	19
Gift Voucher Offer	6	21
Summer Spectacular	6	23
Summer Savers	6	24
Gift with Purchase	7	25
Win a Car Competition	7	27
Summer Sale	8	29
Further Reductions	8	30
Back to School	9	33
Autumn Fashion	9	35
Winter Warmth	10	37
Mid Season Sale	10	39
Gifts for Giving	11	41
Christmas	12	46
Winter Sale	13	49–52

Assignment 10:3 Promotional plans

Take a look at your promotional plans for the current season.

Can you find examples of all 3 types of promotion?

How many of each type are there? Is there scope for more promotional activity to be added?

It is part of the buyer's job to look for sales opportunities. The sales plan and the promotional calendar provide a good starting point. Looking for sales opportunities means identifying the sales peaks and troughs shown in the sales plan and reviewing the existing promotional plans shown on the calendar.

 Promotions can and should be applied to "bend" the sales trend.

Promotional activity should support and enhance the planned sales peaks and stimulate the sales opportunities presented by sales troughs.

Sales Peaks

These present a challenge to the buyer not only to support the planned level of sales volume, but to exceed it. Sales peaks can be natural or engineered. The natural peaks are those which tend to be seasonal, and the engineered peaks are those created by promotional activity. Where the phasing of the sales plan is based on the previous year's sales pattern, these engineered sales peaks may become increasingly difficult to achieve. Promotional plans will need to be strong enough to produce year-on-year sales increases during periods when last year's sales volumes were boosted by promotional activity.

Sales Troughs

These are the periods of low sales volumes in the phased sales plan, which present the buyer with real opportunities for the achievement of sales increases. Creative promotion planning here can bring sales results at times when sales volumes have historically been low.

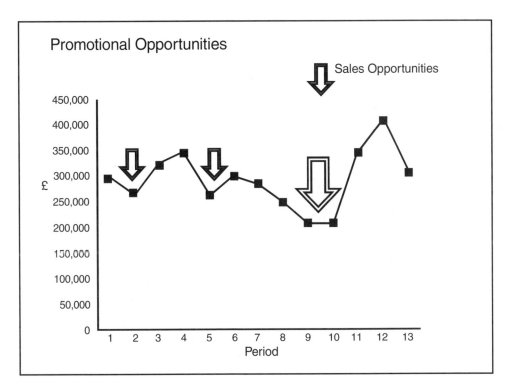

6. Review and Forward Planning

There are undeniably good reasons for reviewing the success of promotional activity. If we can understand the reasons for promotional success or failure, our future planning should benefit from what we have learnt. We should aim for continuous improvement in our planning of successive promotional activities. In the case of each promotion, the objectives should be clearly stated and, wherever possible, quantified so that results can be effectively measured. The results of the promotion should be assessed: *"Did the promotion fulfil its objectives? Was it worth it in sales and gross profit terms?"*

If the answer is *"Yes"*, what made it successful?
If the answer is *"No"*, what made it unsuccessful?

Understanding the reasons for promotional success are just as important as identifying the reasons for failure.

When reviewing promotions, buyers should seek feedback from all those who have an informed opinion (and completely different perspectives) and combine that feedback with the objective analysis available.

The buyer may be tempted to attribute sales success to his/her skill in creating an excellent range, and sales failure to someone else, e.g. the sales staff!

Be careful about the reasons you attribute to the success of any promotion! Try to be as objective as possible.

Let us review the process:

Step 1: Set quantified objectives, e.g. "increase sales by 20%" rather than just "increase sales'.
Step 2: Review results.
Step 3: Identify reasons for success/failure (dig deep!).
Step 4: Specify what you will do differently next time.
Step 5: Apply what you have learnt to your promotional plan for next season.

Assignment 10:4 Reviewing a promotion

Take a recent promotion. Were the objectives clearly stated in advance?

Review the results.

What did you learn: a) from that promotion, specifically?

and b) for future promotional activity, more generally?

Implementation

Whilst planning promotional activity is an analytical and creative process, implementing a successful promotion is an administrative exercise. Effective implementation will depend on early and clear communication of the details to all concerned.

Who needs to know about promotions?

- marketing – to organise advertising
- visual merchandising – to produce point of sale material
- store/department management – to organise the staff to mount the promotion on time.

Time spent on planning promotional activity is likely to result in smoother and quicker operational implementation.

 When it comes to promotions, longer planning time means shorter implementation time.

7. Summary

In this chapter we have considered promotions – their planning, and reviewing results. We have considered promotional objectives and strategy, the customer's purchase motivation and the various types of promotion that can be utilised. We have highlighted the opportunities presented to the buyer in developing tailor made promotions with suppliers, not only to fulfil the retailers scheduled promotional activity, but also to create new promotions for truly incremental sales.

Promotion, in the broadest sense, is about how we present the product to the customer: how we display it, package it and describe it through POS and product labelling. From the buyer's perspective, there are many issues that directly relate to the buyer's role and others that the buyer should at least seek to influence. Presenting the product is the subject of our next chapter.

Checklist

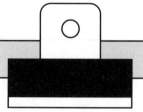

1. Beware of the "busy fools" syndrome; reducing the selling price may cause everyone to work harder and sell more but for no extra profit!

2. If we can understand what motivates the customer to make a purchase, it should be easier to identify the type of promotion most likely to get the best sales results.

3. The best thing to do with old stock is to get rid of it! Old stock ties up the open to buy in the same way as the unsuccessful buy.

4. New product promotion is about selling the features and benefits of the product and is not always accompanied by a consumer price incentive!

5. To become the customers' first choice destination the retailer may need a sustained promotional drive supported by strong advertising support in addition to excellent product ranges.

6. In planning promotions: set objectives, define strategy, consider the motivation to purchase select the promotional method and communicate it!

7. The buyer obviously has a responsibility to provide adequate stock support for any promotional activity to ensure sales optimisation.

8. There is a huge opportunity for the buyer to achieve increased sales and gross profit by securing promotional support from suppliers, financial and conceptual!

9. Promotions can and should be applied to bend the sales trend.

10. Understanding the reasons for promotional success are just as important as identifying the reasons for failure

11. Be careful about the reasons you attribute to the success of any promotion! Try to be as objective as possible.

12. When it comes to promotions, longer planning time means shorter implementation time.

11

Presenting the Product

1. Introduction

In Chapter 10, we looked at the promotion of the product and concluded that promotion, in the broadest sense, is about how we present the product to the customer. Buyers spend most of their energy on the development of their product range before it reaches the store. However, they sometimes forget that how the product is presented to the customer is a critical part in achieving successful sales and overlook issues such as packaging and in-store display.

In this chapter we will consider, from a buying perspective, the in-store presentation of products, how buyers can affect the presentation and the key aspects of visual merchandising which need to be considered.

2. Visual Merchandising from a Buyer's Perspective

The amount of input a buyer will have on the presentation of the product often depends upon the way in which the company is organised. In some organisations, particularly smaller companies, the buyer is responsible for the in-store presentation of the merchandise; in larger companies, the buyers are often involved in the development of layouts which are sent to stores for implementation, and in other companies they may have no input at all!

Given the critical nature of display in affecting the sales performance of the product, it is usually beneficial for a buyer to have some level of involvement. This may involve the need for tact as the buyer may be felt to be encroaching on other people's areas of responsibility. (For example, visual merchandisers may feel that the shop windows are their responsibility, whereas the buyer may want to be involved in their layout, to ensure that the "correct" merchandise is included).

3. Benefits of a Buyer's Involvement in Visual Merchandising

The principle benefit of a buyer being involved in visual merchandising is that the vision which the buyer had during the conception and development of the range is followed through into the store. If this vision is not presented to the customer, then the impact of the range will be lost, the clarity of the offer may become confused and potential sales may not be realised.

This involvement with the store also ensures that the buyer keeps in close contact with the reality of the retail environment and good lessons can be learnt from the experience. For example, the candlesticks which looked great in pink in the supplier's showroom now, on yellow shelves, look rather sickly! The delicate acetate box used for packaging the scarves and which were thought to make stacking easier, disintegrated in-store when the customers insisted on opening the boxes to feel the merchandise. Such lessons can be useful in ensuring that the same mistakes are not repeated and that sales are not consequently lost.

4. Communicating Ideal Presentation Standards

The communication of how the merchandise should be displayed to sales staff becomes more difficult the larger the company, and the greater the distance which exists between buyer and seller. In a small company, the buyer can often speak directly to the sales staff and is frequently on the sales floor. In larger companies, a method is required to ensure that the hundreds of people involved in selling the product understand how it should be presented.

Two main methods are used by larger companies. The first is a general manual covering visual merchandising standards. These detail the methods of display ticketing and pricing, with guidelines about which method to use in different instances and more detailed information such as the correct position of price tickets or swing tags.

The second is a more specific manual (often issued seasonally) which details the actual positioning of the merchandise within the store. Often, such a manual will include layouts and photographs of the product to provide guidance to staff. For example, Courts Furnishers issue a display manual which includes a precise instruction on where specific sizes of showcard should be placed on their bed displays and its implementation is closely monitored in-store. Some companies feel that such manuals are too time consuming to create and too prescriptive to staff, preventing the development of the sales staff's own initiative. However, if a consistent image is required across a large number of stores and the quality of stores staff varies, such a plan can prove invaluable in conveying the vision of the range in store.

Buyers sometimes complain that, despite the issuing of such manuals to store staff, the guidelines are not followed and this can create friction between the buying function and stores. However, the store staff are under increasing pressure and often don't have time to attend to some of the details, which may appear more important to the buyer than the sales staff. Rather than criticising store staff, it is far more productive to look for ways in which their role can be made easier. This may involve the pre-pricing of merchandise before it goes into store, as is common for larger companies such as BhS or Marks and Spencer. Ikea have previously sold fast moving products in dump bins created from the transit box which had a tear-off lid. All the store staff had to do to refill the shelf was to replace an empty dump bin with a full one and tear off the lid!

Look for ways in which the jobs of the sales staff can be made easier by improving the packaging or presentation of products.

5. Packaging

The way in which a product is presented to a customer is as important as the product itself, and packaging forms a critical part of this presentation.

Given this importance, it is essential that a buyer is involved in the development and management of a product's packaging. This involves three key stages:

- identifying the purpose of the packaging
- the packaging policy of the company
- the development process.

 Treat the packaging as part of the product.

a) The Purpose of Packaging

Packaging serves several functions in a retail environment. It will:

- protect the product in transit
- protect the product in store
- communicate the brand
- communicate the product benefits
- enhance the product
- attract the customer.

Any proposed packaging should be given proper consideration in order to ensure that it meets all the relevant functional criteria.

b) Packaging Policy

The way in which the merchandise is presented in store and the packaging policy should link back to the buying strategy and policy. For example, a national chain of convenience stores will often sell packaged products, which are easy for the customer to pick up. An up-market delicatessen will sell many unpackaged products, which are selected and carefully wrapped for the individual customer. Both these companies are reflecting their buying strategy in their approach to packaging – the first is reflecting the strategy of convenience, ease of purchase and speed – while the second, the strategy of individual service, premium products and quality.

Whether a product is sold pre-packaged or not, is a decision which needs to be made during the development of the range. Many buyers forget about the packaging needs of the product until the last minute, but the customer buys the whole offer, not just the product. Think about the way in which you select a gift – the packaging will often influence your choice of purchase.

Whatever the packaging policy of your company, the packaging needs of each product should be determined during the product development stage. This allows for the cost of the packaging to be taken into account, the style of the packaging to be properly considered and the packaging to be produced in time for the product launch.

c) The Development of Packaging

So, how do you go about developing packaging for a product range? Some larger companies are fortunate in that they have a packaging department who can take over this responsibility for the buyer, but in many companies, the buyer will need to organise the design and development of the packaging. Suppliers often become involved in the process and, as it is in their interests that the product sells well, it is always worth asking for their co-operation.

The first stage in developing a product's packaging is to decide what kind of packaging you require. Some products require a cardboard box and others only need a swing ticket. The following list gives some idea of the great choice of options:

- box   - cardboard
  - acetate
  - polypropolene
  - window included
- blister pack
- cardboard tube
- shrink wrap onto card
- polythene bag and header card
- polythene bag
- bottle
- tin
- jar
- sealed plastic bag
- cotton bag
- envelope

The decision as to which type of packaging to use will depend upon the level of protection required by the product, the purpose of the packaging, the company policy with regard to packaging and, possibly, environmental concerns. For example, blister packs are now less commonly used as they are harder to dispose of safely. Now that retailers are responsible for a proportion of this disposal, it is in retailers' interests to take an environmentally friendly approach to their packaging.

Assignment 11:1 Conduct an audit of the type of packaging used within your company.

Consider the following points :

1. Is it consistent throughout the company?

2. What is the purpose of the packaging used?

3. Does the level of information on the packaging and the style of packaging support the buying strategy?

The next stage is to develop a brief for the packaging designer. This brief should provide all the information required for the designer to complete the task and should therefore include:

- the product name to appear on the packaging
- a description of the product   – sizes of product
  - colours
  - any other variables
- retail price if it is to be included on the packaging
- the type of packaging to be used (if known)
- the level of protection required, e.g. does it need to withstand a drop test?
- copy to be included on the packaging or sufficient information to enable a copy writer to produce the copy
- legal information, e.g. country of origin, ingredients, etc.
- guidelines to be followed on   – use of brand
  - typefaces
  - board type
- whether the product is part of a range or to co-ordinate with other packaging.

The clearer the design brief, the easier it will be for the packaging designer and the greater the likelihood that all the packaging within the store will co-ordinate.

 Always check packaging and point of sale copy with people who are not connected with the product to ensure that your message is being communicated effectively.

Set out opposite is an example of a briefing sheet used to brief a designer on the development of the packaging for a camomile shampoo product:

Packaging Brief

Product Name :   Camomile Shampoo

Product description :   Shampoo containing the essence of the herb camomile which will enhance blonde hair and add shine. The product is made with 100% natural ingredients and is not tested on animals.

Size :   250ml

Retail price :   £2.50

Price to appear on packaging :   No

Type of Packaging :   Blue glass bottle with screwtop black lid, dipped in cream wax. Product information to be printed in blue ink onto two self-adhesive kraft paper labels. Front label size 4cm x 8cm, back label size 4cm x 4 cm.

Level of Protection required :   No additional requirements

Copy :   Camomile Shampoo. A natural shampoo to enhance blonde hair. 250ml. This product is not tested on animals. Ingredients : Aqua, Camomile,

Legal Information :   Ingredients

Country of Origin : UK

Guidelines on Use of Brand :   Typeface – Times Roman

Small brand logo - style 3

Brand positioned as per guidelines.

Ink colour : Pantone 536U

Range Information :   The product is a range extension to a current range of shampoo products in store.

6. Method of Presentation

The method of presenting the product in-store should also reflect the company strategy and ensure that the product is merchandised to its maximum benefit. For example, small products are often displayed on large open shelves where they may become muddled and any impact intended by the buyer in their vision of the range becomes lost. A better method is to merchandise smaller products in compartmentalised display units, where each product has its own space.

In many companies, the basic methods of visual merchandising are already established and the buyer can have little impact. However, it is still critical that the buyer considers the method of merchandising when designing the range, to ensure that the product will be compatible with the fixturing. Also, if it is a completely new range, it is important to consider whether the current methods of merchandising will work for the new range. This may lead to requests for new fixtures. Alternatively the buyer may need to make changes to the development of the range. The ability to develop new fixturing will usually depend upon evaluating the cost of the fixturing against the projected sales revenue of the range with and without the new fixturing. Therefore, it is vital to include these costs in any fixturing proposal.

As the buyer is the only person who knows about the ranges being developed, it is therefore the buyer's responsibility to ensure that the product can be effectively merchandised in-store.

 A poorly displayed product range will never achieve its true sales potential.

Methods of Merchandising Products

Many methods of visual merchandising exist. The most common methods are :-

METHOD	USED FOR
• shelves – usually adjustable in height	vases, jumpers, tins
• rails	clothing, paper lanterns
• racks	newspapers, rugs
• freestanding gondola units	as shelves – but with possible promotional use
• pedestals	individual larger products

- compartmentalised units –
  freestanding or to sit on a shelf   cosmetics
- roomsets   furniture

7. Service or Self-service?

The type of service offered by your company will have an impact upon the type of packaging and presentation required. The two extremes of the scale are completely self-service and completely personal service. In a self-service shop the customer has to rely on the information from the packaging and the display to make their decisions. The products will often be pre-packed for convenience and anything which can help to make the customer's purchase decision easier, will help to gain the sale. For example, a carrying handle on a heavy, boxed product will help the customer to realise that the product can easily be carried home. A buyer for a self-service retailer will need to spend more time considering the packaging of the product and ensuring that the presentation is customer friendly. All too often, buyers use technical jargon on packaging, which is meaningless to the customer.

The buyer in a personal service company will often not have to work as hard at the copy on the point of sale material, as shop staff can convey the benefits of the product to the customer. However, they need to ensure that the sales staff are aware of the product's features and benefits and that point of sale material reinforces the service of the sales staff.

A buyer should ensure that the packaging and presentation of the product in-store is compatible with the style of the retailer.

8. Space Efficiency

Retail sites are expensive and it is important that the space gives the maximum return if the company is to be successful. Increasingly, retailers are monitoring the sales generated by the shop space, to assess if the space is working efficiently. The space is usually monitored in terms of sales per square foot (or now, more usually, in square metres). This is calculated by dividing the sales floor into square feet or metres. Each product area, such as a product department, is then entered onto the plan of the sales floor and the total space for the product area is calculated. The total sales of the products within each area are divided by the square meterage of the space, to give the sales per square metre. Some retailers prefer to work with linear metres as they feel that this provides a more accurate reflection of the selling space. The level of detail in which the space efficiency is analysed will often depend upon the company. Some retailers only analyse space efficiency at department level, whilst others go down to individual product level. However, the important consideration when deciding the level of detail required is to decide what you are going to do or are able to do with the information. There is no point spending days getting the last minutiae of detail and then not using the information!

Assignment 11:2 Calculate the sales per square metre for your shop or department.

You may wish to divide the sales area into smaller sections, departments or sub-departments in order to compare their performance. In particular, note the sales near the front and back of the store, and by the till point.

The analysis of sales per square metre should enable a buyer to rank the relative importance of all products or departments from those which have the highest sales per square metre to those with the lowest. Further investigation is then needed to see how the sales per square metre of the lower performing areas, can be increased without having a detrimental effect on the others. Some products may always have a low performance because of their size and value. For example, large, cheap products take up a lot of space but don't necessarily contribute a high turnover or profit. A buyer could discontinue such products from the range, but that may upset the balance of the range and fail to offer the customer the necessary choice.

In some situations, moving or redisplaying the product can increase the sales turnover as is evident from the following case study.

Case History

A retailer in London sold toiletry products as part of their range. Their shelves were very large and went from floor to ceiling. The analysis of the sales per square metre showed that this area had the lowest sales per square metre in the shop.

The company introduced raked shelving units to sit onto the middle shelves. This increased the visibility of the products and permitted the display of a

---

greater variety of product in the same space. Tall bottles were put on the higher, back shelves and small jars were put at the front. The customer could see the products more clearly and access to the products was easier than before.

The very high shelves, which were no longer used for product, were used to create eye-catching displays and signage, to let the customer know what sorts of products were located on the shelves.

In a four week trial, the sales per square metre rose from the lowest to the second highest!

 Before a new product range is introduced consider whether the planned method of presentation will enhance or detract from the product.

9. Layout and Adjacencies

Some buyers will not become involved in the layout of the shopfloor but many do become involved in its planning and it is an important activity to which all buyers should be able to contribute. The buyers are often the only people within the business who can advise on the suitability of proposed product adjacencies because of their knowledge of the product range. For example, a lingerie department space sited next to an open café area could deter female customers by making them feel self-conscious. Changing rooms should be located in quieter areas of the store (so that the customer using the changing room does not feel that they are changing on a motorway), and also so that valuable selling space within the busier areas of the store is not lost.

Customer Flow

One of the most important criteria in the development of the layout of the sales floor is that the customer feels that the customer flow is logical and smooth. The term "customer flow" refers to the direction in which the customer walks around the shop. This will start at the entrance and, hopefully, end at the till. In an ideal world, the customer would have walked around the whole sales floor between these two points and considered the complete product offer.

For example, if a kitchen shop was planned so that the customer moved from chopping boards to knives to mixing bowls to kitchen textiles to tablelinen to serving dishes, the flow would feel logical to the customer.

However, if the flow went from mixing bowls to table-linen to chopping boards to serving dishes to kitchen textiles to knives, the customer could feel confused.

Ikea have developed a reputation for good customer flow, as they direct the customer around the entire store with very few opportunities for deviation. This flow of traffic is by no means accidental and the store layout creates openings and barriers which subtly direct the customer. Signage and walkways can be used to reinforce this route.

Hotspots

The sales floor should never be taken as fixed, as changes to the sales floor or the position of the merchandise can regenerate customer interest and draw attention to special promotions. Large supermarkets will often change around the positioning of merchandise on the shelves in order to ensure that customers consider the entire product offer, rather than just the items on their weekly shopping list. In larger stores, a specific area can be designated to promotions – and "hotspots". Such areas enable merchandise (which is, for example, new or low priced) to be highlighted and can generate a lot of additional business. In smaller stores, this space may not be available for the entire year, but could be created for particular promotions throughout the year.

10. Summary

In this chapter we have considered:

- the presentation of the merchandise in store from the buyer's perspective
- the benefits of good visual merchandise
- the development of packaging and
- the consideration of the shop layout.

The buyer spends considerable time in the development of the range and the vision which they started with can be easily diluted if it is not carried through into the shop or store. This, in turn, can have a negative impact upon sales and lead to a waste of the buyer's efforts. Whilst the in-store environment may not always be the direct responsibility of the buyers, they can, with tact, exert a strong influence, in order to ensure that the customer sees their vision, and that the sales plan for the products is maximised.

Checklist

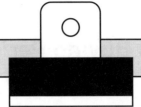

1. *Look for ways in which the jobs of the sales staff can be made easier by improving the packaging or presentation of products.*

2. *Treat the packaging as part of the product.*

3. *Whatever the packaging policy of your company, the packaging needs of each product should be determined during the product development stage. This allows for the cost of the packaging to be taken into account, the style of the packaging to be properly considered and the packaging to be produced in time for the product launch.*

4. *Always check packaging and point of sale copy with people who are not connected with the product to ensure that your message is being communicated effectively.*

5. *A poorly displayed product range will never achieve its true sales potential.*

6. *A buyer should ensure that the packaging and presentation of the product in-store is compatible with the style of the retailer.*

7. *Before a new product range is introduced consider whether the planned method of presentation will enhance or detract from the product.*

12

Improved Buying Performance

1. Introduction

In this final chapter, we will consider what we can do to improve buying performance. We will focus on some specific areas of buying and related activity that, if properly exploited, have the potential to improve the sales performance and the profitability of the retailer.

Buying is inherently risky. Retailing is all about investing in stock speculatively, and hoping it sells! Managing the risk is an important feature within any efficient buying operation, and one to which we will address our attention in this chapter.

Information technology plays an increasingly important role in retail buying as well as in our lives in general. Good information technology (IT) support is essential if a business is to survive in today's retail environment. There are huge potential benefits to be gained from IT systems – and pitfalls too, as we shall see. How we actually operate the business is important, too.

Business process re-engineering became a fashionable term in the business culture of the 1990s. It simply involves a critical review of the way a business operates, and asks, "Are there better ways of doing things?" We will take a look here, at process review.

Finally, in this chapter we will indulge in a little crystal ball gazing, take a look into the future and speculate on the development of retailing in the 21st Century! How will it change? What new challenges will it present? As long as there is retailing, products will have to be bought! The buyer can undoubtedly make a major impact on the profitability and, therefore, the success of a retail organisation. So, let's start by trying to define and describe what makes an effective buyer.

2. The Effective Buyer

All buyers want to do their job well, but what do we mean by being effective and how can this be measured? Ultimately an effective buyer is one who achieves results but the successful buyer is only successful if the products achieve their sales and profit targets – and not just for this season, but year-in and year-out. The achievement of financial targets over the longer term requires considerable skill as well as energy in order to keep producing a winning range. Some companies now move buyers between product areas in order to allow for a fresh approach to the range and to prevent them from becoming stale in their approach. A quick self-check for signs of staleness is to ask how many times you find yourself saying *"we've already tried that"* and *"we can't sell that"*. Some of these reactions may be valid and based upon previous history but customers and markets change over time and, whilst previous history can be helpful, it can also create mental constraints which can be to the detriment of the range.

However, not all a buyer's targets will be financially based. A company may have set targets to increase market share, or to promote an environmental message or, as is sometimes the case with charity retailers, to increase the profile of the charity. Whatever the target, the buyer's ability to achieve the required results will lead to their success or failure.

The criteria for assessment will also be influenced by the style of the company. For example, a discount retailer with a need for high volumes will value a buyer who can negotiate a tough deal rather than a buyer who develops the most aesthetically appealing range. However, for a design-led retailer, the appearance of the range may be paramount.

So, what are the key attributes which make an effective buyer? Interestingly, it is not possible to state one attribute over all others. The buyer's role is complex and relies upon many different attributes of equal ranking.

A good buyer should be *analytical*, although this analysis does not restrict itself to data analysis. Whilst the correct interpretation of reports is important, a buyer must also be able to analyse verbal and visual information, from the shop floor, the marketplace and suppliers.

Communication skills are essential. The buyer will need to communicate with people within their own organisation to ensure that the vision of the range is delivered and also to people *outside* the organisation, such as customers, suppliers or designers. Communication must be effective when written or spoken. The increasing use of e-mail by retailers has lead to a decline in verbal communication in business, but such verbal communication will always remain an essential skill of the buyer.

In order to attain success, a buyer needs to be *pro-active.* A reactive buyer will always be one step behind the competition and only by being pro-active will innovation and market leadership be achieved. This pro-active approach is not only essential for the buyer, but also for the buyer to instil in their staff and their suppliers. It is easier for suppliers to deal with a reactive buyer but better for your business to be pro-active.

Creativity is a key asset. In companies where original product development is undertaken, such creativity is often more obvious and may be supported by a design function. However, the selection and development of any range requires creativity from the buyer. The greater the level of creativity the better the range and the less obvious its elements.

Problems arise every day in a buyer's office, varying from quality issues, to unexpected price increase proposals, late deliveries, too much or too little stock: a myriad of barriers which prevent the buyer from performing their role. The buyer's job is not only to deal with these problems, but also to resolve them, ensuring that they don't reoccur, whilst not forgetting the other aspects of their role while the problems are being resolved. Buyers need to use all their management skills in order to ensure that they **deal with problems** in an effective manner.

Decision-making is a key element of the buyer's role, particularly with regard to range planning. Lots of buyers spend hours considering the options, but then fail to make firm decisions at the end of their deliberations. Worse still, they make a decision and then change their minds!

 Whatever decision you make, stick to it! A focused range will always sell better than one which appears indecisive and unconfident to the customer.

Planning is a critical element of the buyer's role. However, it is frequently given too little consideration and allocated too little time. Consequently the buyer dives into the range development without thinking it through. The end result of such an approach is a poorly considered range and, subsequently, *a poorly performing range.*

Buying is a role that is broader than many management roles. Whereas many managers deal primarily with planning and control, a buyer's role is more extensive and requires the buyer to deal with planning, control, the monitoring of results and reacting. It is therefore both a pro-active and a reactive role. Such breadth makes the role complex and emphasises the need for *a structured and considered approach* in order to achieve success.

The buying process is cyclical – it goes round and round, as long as the company sells products. Part of the buyer's role is to review the performance of the range which has been bought to see if it has sold as anticipated, and to learn lessons with which to make better buying decisions in the future.

As well as reviewing the sales of products it is also beneficial to review the whole approach to buying for the season, as invaluable lessons can be learnt which will improve the buying process in the future.

Assignment 12:1 Performance assessment

A) Use the following questions to assess your performance for the previous season.

• Was the range developed in line with the company strategy and buying policy?

• Were the previous sales performances reviewed?

• Was the range planned properly?

• Was a competition review undertaken?

• Was a supplier appraisal undertaken?

• Was enough time allowed for planning?

• Were the negotiations with suppliers successful?

• Was the vision implemented in store?

• Did the range perform as planned?

• Were all the financial and non-financial targets achieved?

B) Where areas didn't go according to plan try to consider the reasons. Sometimes internal or external factors can prevent a buyer from achieving their goals – these can be called barriers to success. What are the barriers to success in your business?

Answering these review questions at the end of each season can be a painful process if things have not gone as you intended. However, unless you are absolutely honest as to the reasons why things went wrong, you cannot identify an action plan to improve the situation for the next season. Every buyer will be able to identify areas for improvement, but defensive buyers will only back themselves into a spiral of poor performance. Admitting mistakes may not be pleasant, but improving the situation and seeing the benefits can more than compensate.

3. Maintaining an Outward Perspective

Many buyers work in an office environment removed from the sales floor. The increasing level of administration in most buying departments means that it is often difficult to get out of the office into the shops and the competition. This is usually a quick way in which to stop being an effective buyer! The customer, who is the critical element in the business, doesn't sit at the same desk and if you are buying for the customer you need to see what they are seeing. Customers today are far more educated and aware than ever before and, if buyers are to develop ranges to appeal to these customers, then they need to be out and about in the marketplace.

Market research is used by larger retailers to get to know their customers. In reality, the best and most cost-effective way is to go out into the shops and talk to customers. One day on the sales floor will provide the buyer with a substantial amount of information, which will help to improve the range. Some people feel that such anecdotal evidence should not be relied upon, but it often provides a good starting point. Market research, if it can be afforded, could then be used to obtain greater information with which to corroborate the initial findings.

Market research can also be effective in obtaining direct feedback from customers. This can be achieved by exit interviews in store or by focus groups, which allow for more in-depth investigation. The key to getting the most out of market research is to know what you want to achieve and then to brief the market research company accordingly. If the brief is vague and non-specific, then so will be the results.

Feedback can come from many sources, some formal – like market research – and some informal. Conversations with customers in-store, feedback from colleagues and senior managers can all provide valuable insight. Sometimes a buyer can become too close to the range and a single comment from a colleague or customer can help to regain the clarity. In order to receive such valuable feedback, a buyer has to be receptive and openness is a valuable asset.

Most buyers think of their customers as being the people who buy the product in the shops. However, a broader definition would include the internal teams who support the buyers. A large buying office will often have internal support functions such as design, packaging, quality control, in-store graphics, visual merchandising, marketing and stores, as well as external interfaces with suppliers, shipping companies and agents. In order for the buying process to be effective, buyers must be able to manage all these interfaces and ensure that their activities assist these other departments in the undertaking of their roles.

A key danger of working with so many other departments can be that the buyer becomes too involved in other people's jobs, to the detriment of the buyer's own work. In order to avoid this danger, buyers need to ensure that they concentrate upon their own objectives and develop awareness for the projects to which they can add value or that will add value to their role. If an interface with another department is not working, a solution needs to be found, but this will very rarely involve the buyer taking over the responsibility for the additional role.

4. Improving Performance

The first stage to address in improving productivity is to decide exactly what you are looking to improve.

- At the simplest level it may be sales turnover; however, it may be that sales turnover is very high but profitability is poor. In this instance the buyer would look to improve profits whilst not decreasing sales
- It may be that stockturn is too low and, by negotiating lower minimum quantities per order and increasing sales, then stock turn can be increased
- Sales in larger stores may be the same value as in the smaller stores, causing the company to investigate sales or profit productivity, otherwise known as the sales or profit density (i.e. sales per square metre).

Solutions to such improvement targets will rarely be simple and will often involve a review encompassing suppliers, stores and systems. The first step has to be to collate all the known information. The more informed the buyer is about the exact situation, the better the solution.

In order to be effective, the buyer needs to accumulate and use a large amount of information. Using the information is a critical part of the process; otherwise it may be as much use as a closed library!

The typical information amassed by a buyer should cover:

- the competition
- the market
- supply base
- production techniques
- production costs
- origination costs
- production limitations

- detailed knowledge of the product range
- the economic climate
- freight and duty rates for imported goods and current movements in these prices
- raw commodity prices, e.g. steel, pulp or cotton
- lead times
- product prices
- product sales.

All this information should be used to ensure that the buyer's targets are achieved and that improvements, which are required from the range, are achieved. For example, knowledge of production techniques can lead to the buyer suggesting more economical ways of producing the product and thereby achieving a lower cost price (this might be needed to increase the profitability or competitiveness of the product).

Many buyers are very capable when it comes to facts and figures. Truly gifted buyers are able to add that bit extra which includes flair and vision.

Flair comes in the creative development of the range and covers, not just individual products, but the way in which the whole range is created and presented. Such ranges can excite and stimulate the customer who is always looking for something different and this will usually lead to increased sales.

Vision starts with the planning of the range and goes right through to its implementation in-store. This vision, as we stated in Chapter 2, is often lost in-store when the range is merchandised by people who do not understand the buyer's original vision and, not surprisingly, find that they can't implement it.

Such flair and vision is very hard to teach, which is why it is so valuable to a business. However, by starting the range development process with a vision – and keeping this at the forefront of your mind – by being willing to consider the non-obvious as well as the obvious products and to think "out of the box", such flair will be nurtured.

 The most obscure products can be considered during the range development process, as it's easier to pull back from the more obscure than it is to introduce the more dramatic at the end of the development process.

A buyer's skill is built over many years. Whilst it cannot be denied that some people have a natural flair for buying, this flair needs to be combined with experience to develop it into real skill. Likewise, intuition or "gut feel" has helped many buyers, but this needs to combine with experience to enable it to become commercial judgement. Some people think that good buyers are born and not made. In reality, good buyers are both!

Creativity, as we have stated earlier, is a key attribute of high achiever buyers – either in their development of the product range or in their approach to solving problems. Some buyers are fortunate to work within a creative environment, surrounded by like-minded people. However, many buyers work on their own in a small office, and creativity can seem hard to attain. In such situations, certain techniques can be used to develop creativity. Although others within the business may not understand the methods, they will appreciate the results.

If buyers stare at the same wall every day, they will not be at their most creative. A change of scene (by going to see a supplier or a trade fair) can free up the mind and lead to clearer thoughts. The interaction with other people also provides the opportunity for problems or ideas to be aired. Some buyers feel that sharing their problems with a supplier is a sign of weakness, but most suppliers, who are as interested in the success of the business as the buyer, react more positively and are happy to express their opinions.

Brainstorming

Brainstorming is a recognised technique to encouraging creative thought, either by yourself or, even better, with other people involved in the buying process. Start with a large sheet of paper and write down at random all the thoughts which arise on the issue in question. Do not try to edit at this stage – that can come later – and thoughts which are not expressed can clog up the brain. It is vital that brainstorming is seen as a relaxed and non-competitive activity; for this reason, many businesses will conduct brainstorming outside the work environment or over a glass of wine!

Once the thoughts have all been noted down, judgement is needed to assess which ideas are innovative, practical and feasible given the constraints of your business, such as time or budget. A work programme can then be developed to ensure that the benefits of the brainstorm are not lost.

Jargon phrases can come and go, but "thinking out of the box" is a worthwhile phrase for every buyer. The "box" is essentially all those elements which can constrain a buyer and can include:

- a set view of the customer – *"Our customer's wouldn't buy that."*
- a narrow view of the product range – *"We can't sell that."*
- budgetary constraints – *"We can't afford to do that"*, and many more.

Whilst some of these constraints may be valid, a buyer who works within them will only develop the obvious range, which may fail to inspire the customer. Constraints will be imposed at a later stage, but during the development process, they should be pushed to the background and not left in the foreground.

5. Managing Risk

Do you like taking risks or do you like to play it safe? Some people are born risk-takers whilst others are naturally more cautious: but being a buyer is all about taking risks. Buying is risk!

Every product the buyer purchases (unless it is specifically ordered for a customer) is bought speculatively, destined to sit on the shelf or rail, until a customer comes along to buy it!

To what extent should retailers expose themselves in terms of stock investment? Let's think the process through:

Stock is bought in anticipation of sales. Our stock investment at any one time is the sum total of our existing stockholding and our forward commitment, or orders. Buying product ranges six months ahead exposes the retailer to risk – a risk that is compounded if the current stock investment is also high. Heavy forward stock commitment injects inflexibility into the buying process. If an attractive new purchase opportunity presents itself, we may not be able to take advantage of it if there is heavy forward commitment to stock. Of course, buyers do not have complete control over buying lead times; the market in which the buyer operates often dictates them. How then, can the buyer manage the risk?

Within most product ranges, whether it's fashion or furniture, there is relatively safe product and relatively high-risk product. Safe products are the core, basic lines that are always in demand. From the retailer's point of view, this is stock that never needs to be marked down, it never goes out of fashion, and it is an easy profit earner. High-risk products can be seasonal or fashionable, and consumer demand for them will pass. From the retailer's point of view, these are stock lines that will need to be marked down if they remain unsold after a prescribed period. Because it is high-risk stock that is likely to attract markdown action, it will often carry a higher planned margin.

That's not to say that safe is good. A department full of bestsellers would probably look decidedly boring!

Example

About 75-80% of handbag sales come from 2 colours: black and navy. These are the best selling colours. If the best selling handbag styles in a range were identified and all ranged in the best selling colours, you would have an assortment of best sellers ... that would look awful! In this example, it is the more peripheral colours and styles that add interest to the range. They may not sell as fast as the "basics" but they collectively give the range credibility and, importantly, visual appeal.

The point is, there is a balance to be achieved.

The amount of high-risk stock, as a proportion of the range, needs to be kept in check.

A responsive open to buy system driven by a realistic sales forecast would provide certain levels of open to buy that should not be over-spent. However, it is worth noting that the buyer can become "over-bought" either by directly overspending if management controls fail to prevent it, or simply by failing to achieve the sales target. Stock commitment could be within the available open to buy one day, and then over-bought the next when actual results are reported, or the forecast is reviewed. The goal posts keep moving!

To manage risk – work within the open to buy.

Sale or return arrangements with the supplier remove the risk from the retailer. If the product or range fails to sell within the prescribed period, it goes back to the supplier. There is usually an initial stock investment when, at the outset, the stock is bought in the usual way, but the retailer has the benefit of sales without the *commitment* to stock.

"Bank stock" or "Pay on Sale" arrangements operate in a similar way. In a bank stock arrangement, the supplier funds the stock investment, with the retailer paying for the stock only as it is sold. The retailer has the benefit of the sales without the stock investment.

Deferred payment deals will be of benefit to the retailer but may not always reflect in the buyer's performance results. Whether the buyer is able to claim credit for the benefit to the business which will accrue from deferred payment deals, will depend on the accounting and reporting methods that are employed. Deferred payment arrangements are of benefit to the cash flow of the business. Stock is ordered and delivered, but payment is postponed for an extended period beyond the normal settlement period. For instance, the normal settlement period might be 30 days, but a deferred payment deal might allow for payment to be delayed for 60 days, giving a 90-day credit period in total. The benefit to the buyer is that the goods can be brought into the business early in the season and in bulk, providing an opportunity to sell the majority of the stock before payment becomes due.

A deferred payment deal may enable a stronger merchandise presence earlier in the season than would have otherwise been possible.

6. Systems and Processes

Information Technology has to interface with business processes. This will often mean a change or, at least, a review of the way things are done. Information Technology can deliver enormous benefits and cost savings to a retail organisation. It can also represent an enormous cost if not linked to business process improvements. It is important to establish what we expect of our IT systems – relevant information delivered with speed and accuracy.

This means defining what is *relevant* and identifying where the raw data will come from.

When deciding what information you need to run an efficient buying (and selling) operation, it is important to establish what you will do with the information when you have it. Will it fall into the "interesting but useless" category, or is it information that will prompt decision-making? In order to establish your information *needs,* as opposed to desires or aspirations, you should ask yourself what you would do with the information on receipt. What action will it prompt or what decisions will it facilitate? This is what separates data from information – its usefulness!

Smart organisations demand more information, less data!

There are a variety of computer software packages available offering everything from complete merchandising systems to individual modules to fulfil different aspects of the buying function, designed to interface with existing systems.

Expert technical advice and support will be necessary in assessing the compatibility of systems solutions with business needs. Identifying business needs is a critical first step.

There are systems that can provide profitability information down to product level. For example, Direct Product Profitability (DPP), where costs associated with warehousing, transport and stock distribution can be apportioned to each product line. Whilst this information holds an obvious attraction for the buyer, there is a real danger of information overload. There could easily be a situation where there is so much information, it becomes impossible to review it or, more importantly to react to it.

 Beware of analysis paralysis!

Linked to, but separate from the need for quality Information Technology support is the need for efficient processes. A critical review of processes is required whenever there is a change to IT systems; the two are closely inter-related. A good way of doing this is to compile a flow chart of the process under review. This would show the direction of information flow and the inter-dependency of all critical steps in the process. Using this method, a process can be mapped and reviewed, making it easier to decide whether there is a better way of doing whatever it is you are trying to achieve.

In the sample flow chart shown overleaf, a customer order cancellation process is being mapped. It tracks the process from the point where the customer initiates cancellation and shows the response process from the store through to the Distribution Centre (referred to as the DC).

Flow Chart
Customer order cancellation

Where is cancellation request received?

Store → DC

1. Salesperson confirms customer's details, order no., payment to date, and whether the goods have been delivered.
2. Refund given to the customer.
3. EPOS order updated.

DC refer the customer to the **store** in all circumstances. DC CANNOT authorise customer cancellations.

Where is the order being supplied from?

Free stock **(DC)** / Supplier **(MTO)**

Where are the goods now?

At DC / *With the customer* / *With the customer* / *Where are the goods now?* / *With the supplier*

Store cancel the order. **DC** provide a Cancellation Reference.

Store arrange order cancellation & uplift of goods by **DC.**

Store cancel the order. **DC** provide a Cancellation Reference.

Can the order be cancelled?

At DC

Yes / *No*

DC collect the goods from the customer.

Store cancel the order and obtain reference.

Supplier despatches item to **Store**, NOT **DC.**

DC Quality Control

Store sell item.

Item returned to Free Stock.

Item repaired or scrapped.

Item returned to **supplier.**

Item despatched to **store** for sell-off.

Store raise AOC for credit. Copy to **supplier** and copy to **DC.**

DC = Distribution Centre

206

7. The Way Forward

Current Developments in the Market

Retailing is an increasingly fast moving and ever changing industry and this changeability affects all those involved, including buyers. One of the best ways to deal with change is to embrace it, as resisting change can often prove futile. Detailed in the next section are some of the key changes that are affecting the retail industry today.

Home Shopping

The busier lifestyle of customers which restricts their time for shopping, the increased use of electronic commerce on the internet and the restrictions on high street space which prevent retailers from expanding, have all led to the increase in *home shopping*. This change of selling environment has led to buyers having to consider many new areas such as how the benefits of their product can be communicated to the customer, the minimum value of products within the range (for example, will customers bother to order and pay for delivery on a product costing 99p?) and the logistical implications of transporting the product to the customer's home. The ease of home shopping has also led customers to expect more from their in-store experience, either in the range of additional services offered such as a "carry to car" service, home delivery or special orders – or a greater level of interaction with sales staff. Buyers now need to consider not only the products that they sell, but also the services which support the product.

No one who has been in business over the last ten years can have failed to notice the increasing use of *computers* within the buyer's role. Ten years ago, buyers did not have easy access to a computer. Now virtually every buyer has a PC on his or her desk and needs to be proficient in its use.

Spreadsheets, e-mail and systems reports can make buyers' lives easier, but they can also drown a buyer in paperwork. The skill is therefore to make the computer work for you rather than the other way round! The best way to achieve this is both to have good computer skills, which allow the most efficient and effective use of the computer, and also to know exactly what answers you are looking to the computer to provide.

 Remember, however good the computer, it is only one of many valuable tools available to the buyer and can never replace the buyer's knowledge and skill.

Any review of the UK retail market will reveal that we live in dynamic and changing times and it is not just retail which is changing, but the *customers* as well.

On average, Britain's consumers are now older, more informed and better off than in previous decades. Changes to income, age and expectations have led to many lifestyle changes which have impacted upon the retailer. For example, the decline of traditional Sunday lunch and a more casual approach to dining has led to sales moving from formal to casual tableware. This more informal approach to living is also reflected in a move towards casual dressing. Think how many companies now allow casual dress every day when suits were the norm. Such changes are important for retailers, and particularly for buyers, who have to reflect current lifestyle trends in their product ranges.

The good news for the retail industry is that the buying role is becoming more *professional*. More buyers are undertaking formal training, and undergraduate and postgraduate degrees in retailing are now available. A more structured approach is being taken to range planning and management, and consequently a different type of person is being attracted to the role.

The days of the "prima donna buyer" and four-hour lunches are now part of retail history. Buyers are now expected to be "hands-on" in their role and, with the increasing availability of PCs, administration in all sizes of company is increasingly being undertaken by the buyer, rather than by myriad assistants. This increased professionalism has also meant that buyers are more flexible and a large company can now move its buyers to where they are needed – armed with procedural rather than product knowledge.

Most buyers also find that the role is expanding in its responsibilities. There is an increasing number of people with whom to liaise – from stores to marketing to suppliers – to ensure that the vision for the range is translated into the branches or stores. In order that this additional pressure does not lead to becoming over-stressed and ineffective, the buyer now has to learn to manage the role – prioritising tasks for maximum effectiveness.

8. Summary

Buying is a complex and challenging role, but also one which is personally rewarding. Little can beat the feeling of seeing a customer buy a product you have developed or selected – or the buzz when the products achieve their sales targets. Unfortunately such "highs" come with "lows" and things will not always go to plan.

We hope that this book has offered some guidance, to enable you to achieve those highs and minimise the lows of being a retail buyer.

In Part 1 of this book we reviewed buying and merchandising as a function within retailing and examined the various aspects of buying policy.

In Part 2, we went on to look at buying techniques in some detail, starting with planning the budget and range structure to provide the foundation for the buyer's sourcing, product selection and development activity.

Having completed the buying cycle, we considered, in Part 3, promotion and presentation of the product and, critically, the review of performance that should lead to improvements in productivity and profitability.

In this last chapter, we have examined the key factors for the achievement of improved buying performance. Certainly, the personal skill and judgement of the buyer cannot be under-estimated. Buyers are valued by prospective employers for their knowledge, experience, track record and supplier contacts: a new buyer will often introduce the retailer to new sources of supply.

Achieving an improved buying performance is not always easy. What makes buying difficult is the number of variables the buyer has to cope with – not least, the very unpredictable nature of sales!

Retailing operates in a vigorous, dynamic and uncertain environment. The challenge presented to the buyer is to keep pace with it!

Checklist

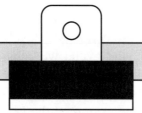

1. Whatever decision you make, stick to it. A decisive range will always sell better than one which appears indecisive and unconfident to the customer.

2. The most obscure products can be considered during the range development process, as it's easier to pull back from the more obscure than it is to introduce the more dramatic at the end of the development process.

3. The amount of high-risk stock as a proportion of the range needs to be kept in check.

4. To manage risk – work within the open to buy.

5. A deferred payment deal may enable a stronger merchandise presence earlier in the season than would have otherwise been possible.

6. Smart organisations demand more information, less data!

7. Beware of analysis paralysis!

8. Remember – however good the computer, it is only one of many valuable tools available to the buyer and can never replace the buyer's knowledge and skill.

9. Retailing operates in a vigorous, dynamic and uncertain environment. The challenge presented to the buyer is to keep pace with it!

APPENDICES

Appendix 1

Answers to the Questionnaire on page 110

1. A buyer's relationship with a supplier should be:

		1	2	3	4
a)	Adversarial	☐	☐	☐	✖
b)	Relaxed and friendly	☐	☐	✖	☐
c)	A professional partnership	✖	☐	☐	☐
d)	As determined by the supply base policy	☐	✖	☐	☐

A buyer should have a professional relationship with suppliers based upon their mutual commitment to the achievement of sales and profits. This relationship will be determined by supplier base policy and an over friendly or over aggressive relationship will not prove effective for either party.

2. How is the supply base best managed?

		1	2	3	4
a)	By regular meetings with suppliers	☐	✖	☐	☐
b)	By a formal process of supplier evaluation	✖	☐	☐	☐
c)	By the supply base management team	☐	☐	✖	☐
d)	By ad-hoc reviews	☐	☐	☐	✖

Formal and structured evaluation of suppliers will provide an objective assessment of their performance. Regular meetings will reinforce this assessment, as can the work of supply base management. An ad-hoc approach is unlikely to prove effective.

3. A new supplier may be found by?

		1	2	3	4
a)	Looking in trade journals	☐	✖	☐	☐
b)	Word of mouth	☐	☐	✖	☐
c)	Advertising	☐	☐	☐	✖
d)	Trade fairs	✖	☐	☐	☐

The sources of new suppliers are many and various. Trade fairs and journals may prove the most reliable methods, although word of mouth can be effective. Advertising is possible, but could be seen as a rather desperate measure.

4. Which of the following points are important to include in a supplier evaluation?

		1	2	3	4
a)	The supplier's delivery record	☐	✖	☐	☐
b)	How much you like the personnel	☐	☐	✖	☐
c)	The quality of the product	✖	☐	☐	☐
d)	How often they take you to lunch	☐	☐	☐	✖

Whether delivery or quality is rated the higher will depend upon the buying policy, however, both would usually be included in a supplier evaluation. Personal preferences or the extent of their hospitality should be irrelevant.

5. A retailer may decide to buy direct from an overseas source because?

		1	2	3	4
a)	The retailer has more control over the product development	☐	☐	✖	☐
b)	The buyers like to travel	☐	☐	☐	✖
c)	The products are cheaper	✖	☐	☐	☐
d)	They have their own import department	☐	✖	☐	☐

Buying direct from an overseas source can offer better prices and more control over product development, but importation needs to be managed and has its own cost implications. Anyone who sees buyer's sourcing trips as holidays are sadly deluded.

6. A buyer can be successful in negotiation by:

		1	2	3	4
a)	Only conceding a point when offered something in return	☐	☐	✖	☐
b)	Preparing thoroughly	☐	✖	☐	☐
c)	Allowing the supplier to control the agenda	☐	☐	☐	✖
d)	Working towards a win-win scenario	✖	☐	☐	☐

Successful negotiation should lead to a win-win scenario where both retailer and supplier are happy with the outcome. Preparation will help to achieve this, as will only offering concessions in return for a concession. Allowing the supplier to control the agenda is unlikely to lead to success.

Appendix 2

Reading List

Selling and Sales Management

Law for Retailers	Bill Thomas, Management Books 2000, 1997
Retail Buying	Diamond and Pintel, Prentice Hall
Managing Retail Sales	Peter Fleming, Management Books 2000, 1998
Retail Selling	Peter Fleming, Management Books 2000, 1995
Retail Marketing	Peter McGoldrick, McGraw Hill, 1990
A Passion for Excellence	Tom Peters, Collins, 1985
The Profession of Selling (series)	John Fenton, Management Books 2000, 1998
The Richer Way	Julian Richer
Cases in Retail Management	Peter McGoldrick, Pitman

Negotiating Skills

Successful Negotiating in a Week	Peter Fleming, Hodder & Stoughton, 1998
Negotiating the Better Deal	Peter Fleming, International Thomson Press, 1997

Leadership and Team-building

The Action–Centred Leader	John Adair, Kogan Page, 1988
Common Sense Leadership	Roger Fulton,Ten Speed Press, 1995
Leadership and the One-minute Manager	K Blanchard, Fontana/ Collins,1988
The One-Minute Manager Builds High Performing Teams	K Blanchard, Harper/Collins, 1996
Positive Leadership	Mike Pegg, Management Books 2000, 1994
Team Management	Charles Margerison and Dick McCann, Management Books 2000, 1995

Appendix 3

BSSA Courses

The British Shops and Stores Association produces an annual training programme with the sole aim of developing the competence and skills of retail staff and proprietors, particularly where selling, buying, and management is concerned. Many of these programmes complement the contents of this book; however, those listed below will be of particular relevance.

Managing Customer Service Workshop

Workshop Profile
The 2-day event is designed for all Managers who need to create effective customer care teams and improve business results.

Learning objectives:
- Recognise and enhance factors which contribute to the business image
- Organise improvements in customer awareness and maximise selling opportunities
- Create motivated teams to provide high quality customer service
- Create improved customer awareness and maximise selling opportunities
- Lead their teams effectively with a workable management style
- Manage difficult customer situations.

Managing Customer Service Workshop

Workshop Profile

A 3-day workshop designed to help managers improve their "bottom lines" through re-examining their retail planning and controlling skills.

Learning objectives:
- Identify critical success factors in retail business
- Analyse current sales and profit performance
- Recommend an improvement plan
- Consider the productive use of resources and how this could be improved
- Propose a development plan for future trading growth
- Avoid poor operational management.

Oxford Summer School

School Profile
A 7-day residential school led by keynote speakers and tutorials incorporating syndicate exercises on topics from buying and merchandising to business finance and store layout.

Learning Objectives:
- Analyse profit and loss accounts
- Generation of cash flow
- Decision-making on stock, sales and orders

- Develop and effective management style
- Present a new store opening plan
- Prepare a complete 5-year profit profile.

Retail Management Open Learning Course

Course Profile
This course develops the skills of those with management potential to strive for greater competence in the management of their business.

Learning Objective:
- Approaches to management, i.e. systems, scientific
- Fundamentals of management, i.e. planning, policies
- Accounting methods
- Motivation, communication, delegation

Further information is available from BSSA at Middleton House, Main Road, Middleton Cheney, Oxon., OX17 2TN (Telephone 01295-712277 or Facsimile 01295-711665).

Appendix 4

Other books in this series

RETAIL SELLING
How to Achieve Maximum Sales
by Peter Fleming
(192 pages, £12.99)

The first book in the series, this is a practical guide for all retail salespeople. It shows you how to improve your sales and increase customer satisfaction.

With more than 100 performance tips, 14 case histories, 16 assignments and 11 self-test questionnaires, this book is really a complete training course in just 192 pages. Every retail salesperson should have a copy.

'This book gives the sales person a great opportunity to develop key skills which will help them achieve success in this crucial job. I have no hesitation in recommending it to you.' *Tim Daniels, Managing Director, Selfridges*

LAW FOR RETAILERS
The Legal Beagle Sets You Straight
by Bill Thomas
(224 pages, £12.99)

The second in the series, this is a practical guide for retail managers, salespeople and shop assistants – in fact, anyone concerned with the day-to-day business of dealing with retail customers and/or suppliers.

The book gives detailed advice on all aspects of retailers' legal obligations to both customers and suppliers, and what to do in the event of legal action by any of the parties concerned.

'This book is essential reading for everyone in the retail trade. It is a unique guide, charting a practical course through the labyrinth of legal pitfalls and stumbling blocks with which every retailer is familiar. Read this book and you may save yourself a considerable amount of time, money – and worry.'
Allan Sayers, Chief Executive, BSSA

MANAGING RETAIL SALES
How to Lead and Motivate the Sales Team
and Manage the Retail Business
by Peter Fleming
(192 pages, £12.99)

The third book in the series, this is a guide for managers. It covers all aspects of retail store management, including sections on team leadership, recruitment and staff development, creating the right sales environment, customer care, stock control, health and safety and security.

Like the another books in this series it is packed with performance tips, case histories, assignments and self-test questionnaires. It will provide an essential reference both for new managers and for seasoned hands.

'Managing a retail business becomes more demanding year by year. I welcome Peter Fleming's most recent book for newly appointed and experienced managers.' *Peter Still, Managing Director, John Lewis Partnership*

To order, phone Management Books 2000 on 01285-760722; credit card orders accepted on VISA or Access.

Index

Commitment, 161
Communication, 13, 182
   costs, 106
   skills, 195
Community issues, 38
Company strategy, 188
Competition, 26-27, 116, 198
Competitors' ranges, 99
Complaints policy, 43, 53
Computers, 207
Concession business, 50
Constraints, 202
Consumer
   demand, 50
   incentives, 174
   interest, 168
   objections, 39
Contract, 108
Convenience, 184
Convenience stores, 184
Core ranges, 118
Corporate personality, 37
Corporate strategy, 15, 21, 23
Cost prices, 34
Cost recovery, 123
Costs and pricing, 132
Creativity, 196
Current developments, 207
Current trading, 144
Customer, 26, 28-29, 208
   appeal, 80
   base, 30
   flow, 191
   issues, 41
   loyalty, 132
   profiles, 29, 30-31, 41
   service, 44
   traffic, 165, 167
   types, 30
Customs & Excise, 105

Dead stock, 52
Decision-making, 196
Deferred payment, 204
   terms, 35
Delivery
   arrangements, 36
   late, 43
Demographic profiling, 41
Demonstration videos in-store, 172
Department store, 58
Design-led retailer, 195
Designers, 120
   briefing, 186

Differentiation, 131
Direct approaches, 99
Direct importing, 104
Direct product profitability, 205
Direct sales response, 168
Discount retailer, 195
Discounting, 35, 45
Display
   methods, 27
   stock, 92
   units, 188
Distress purchases, 167
Distribution centre, 205
Dual pricing, 46
Dump bin, 183
Duty, 105

E-commerce, 207
Economic survival, 41
Effective buyer, attributes of, 195
Environmental issues, 40, 195
Ethical stance, 40
Evolution or revolution, 41
Excellence, establishing, 169
Exit interviews, 198
Extended credit, 170

Facings, 85
Fashion
   accessories, 151
   element, 118
   ranges, 118
   retailers, 115, 118
Feasibility, 121
Feedback, 198
Financial
   budget, 57-58
   objectives, 28
   planning, 58
   targets, 195
Fit, 43
Fixturing, 36, 85, 188
Flair, 200
Floor area, 85
   layout plan, 89
FOB, 105
Focus groups, 29, 198
Footfall, 167, 169
Forecasting, 161
Forward planning, 178
Free offers: buy two, get one free, 170
Freight costs, 105
Friction, 183